HEAVEN IS ON ITS FEET

HEAVEN IS ON ITS FEET

by

Billy Joe & Sharon Daugherty

Heaven Is on Its Feet
ISBN 1-56267-076-X
Copyright © 1999 by
Billy Joe & Sharon Daugherty
Victory Christian Center
7700 South Lewis Avenue
Tulsa, OK 74136-7700

CONTENTS

INTRODUCTION

God's last-day Church, the Church of the Lord Jesus Christ, the Church of this hour, will not leave the earth to be caught up with Jesus as a defeated, weak, or selfish Church.

On the contrary, it will be a Church of mighty victors — men and women and boys and girls of valor — a Church of service and compassion, willing to lay down its life for every race, nation, kindred, tongue, and people (Revelation 14:6). Involvement in worldwide revival will be center stage in its purpose for being.

The Church is not a structure. It is *people*. God's heartbeat is *people*. As God's people, we need to have the same love, compassion, care, and concern for one another as a single Body, and secondly, have the compassion of Christ to daily pull others from the kingdom of darkness (Satan's realm) into the Kingdom of Light (the Kingdom of God's dear Son)!

To be effective in this last hour of the Church age, we must know who we are in Christ and understand His love for us as a creation of God before we can reach out to others with His love.

We must have an attitude of authority, or what I call a "possessing the land mentality," to live in daily victory and triumph in Christ, as He ordained, to take from the enemy by force the people and possessions he has illegally taken, and to maintain a stance of victory and triumph. The weapons of force God has given us are the Word, the blood, the name of Jesus, and His Spirit.

We must be alert to the promises as well as the perils of the last-day Church of Jesus Christ so we can walk in wisdom in this hour. Many believers have been so oriented to the benefits, blessings, and rewards of the Kingdom of God that they have forgotten what God has called them to do. In some instances, a "gimme," materialistic attitude in the Church runs a parallel to that which is in the world.

In this book, my wife Sharon presents two chapters that clearly delineate the promises and perils of the hour we are in.

The victorious last-day Church of Jesus Christ must eat the strong meat of the Word and be willing to become teachers rather than remain babies. We must commit ourselves to a life of daily prayer to develop a strong, intimate relationship with the Father, Son, and Holy Spirit.

As mighty men and women, we must possess a Timothy heart, which is a heart of submission, obedience, diligence, and commitment to the Lord Jesus Christ and to those in authority over us. Our hearts must be sensitive, caring, and compassionate for our brothers and sisters in the Lord and for the lost.

The last-day Church must be led by the Holy Spirit — not by the whims or traditions of men.

Jesus said, **"He who is greatest among you shall be your servant"** (Matthew 23:11). The mighty men and women, boys and girls, of the last-day Church will be those who are free of selfishness and are willing to serve — giving their all for the purposes of the Kingdom of God! Jesus is our ultimate example of a servant. We are to follow the model He established for us.

There is a cost for serving in God's Kingdom, but the rewards far outweigh the cost. Jesus didn't hide the cost of discipleship. He didn't talk only of the good things that will happen to you as His disciple. In this book, I have attempted to bring a balance to the joys of discipleship as well as the cost.

Today is the day to accept your role in the Kingdom of God. If you've missed it, you can get back on track!

It's time to live for Christ that we may please Him who enlisted us as soldiers (2 Timothy 2:4). It's the hour to **"...lay aside every weight, and the sin which doth so easily beset us, and let us run with patience the race that is set before us, looking unto Jesus the author and finisher of our faith..."** (Hebrews 12:1,2 KJV).

The motive of this book is to awaken you, as Joel prophesied, and help you arise as mighty men and women, boys and girls, spiritually prepared to assume your role in God's last-day Church.

> **Prepare for war! Wake up the mighty men...Put in the sickle, for the harvest is ripe.... Multitudes, multitudes in the valley of decision! For the day of the Lord is near in the valley of decision.**
>
> **Joel 3:9,13,14**

This is the hour to step into position in the rank to which the Father has called *you*! Let's go after the hurting and the lost. In Christ, we can make a difference!

Billy Joe Daugherty

1

HEAVEN IS ON ITS FEET

In January 1996, as I was preparing to speak at a men's breakfast meeting, the Spirit of God came on me in an unusual way. I began to convulse and tears poured from my eyes as I caught a vision of being surrounded by a great cloud of witnesses.

The moment the Holy Spirit came on me, I turned to Hebrews 12:1,2 and read:

> **Therefore we also, since we are surrounded by so great a cloud of witnesses, let us lay aside every weight, and the sin which so easily ensnares us, and let us run with endurance** [*The King James Version* says **"patience"**] **the race that is set before us,**
>
> **Looking unto Jesus, the author and finisher of our faith, who for the joy that was set before Him endured the cross, despising the shame, and has sat down at the right hand of the throne of God.**

In the fourth quarter of a pro football game when the two-minute warning is given, and particularly when the score is close, the crowd stands spontaneously to its feet and begins to cheer. I sensed the "cloud of witnesses" on their feet, cheering us on in our spiritual race.

As Bruce Mow led the men at the breakfast meeting in

worship and praise, he stopped and spoke the exact words I was thinking about the great cloud of witnesses, totally unaware how the Spirit of God was dealing with me. He said, "Men, there is a great cloud of witnesses surrounding us. It is time to lay aside every sin and weight that has tripped us up." The thought kept coming to me, *Heaven is on its feet!*

We are in the final part of the race, in the last of the last days. Maybe you have never thought about the people in heaven in an arena watching while you are on the track. They aren't sitting back with arms folded. They are on their feet, shouting, "Go for it!"

Jesus is interceding for you and me right now, and we are surrounded by a great cloud of witnesses who started something which we are to finish. I can assure you, they are interested in whether we reach the goal that is set before us!

We are beginning a new millennium. Six thousand years of humans on the earth is marked in this season of time.

Second Peter 3:8 says, **"With the Lord one day is as a thousand years, and a thousand years as one day."** In this sense, we have come to the end of six days. So what will happen on the seventh day? It is the belief of most conservative evangelical Bible theologians that there will be a seventh day of sabbath rest, which is the millennial reign of Jesus Christ.

People have estimated that our calendar could be off

four to seven years either way. I'm not a date setter, but I want to know the times and seasons of what is going on spiritually. We are in the season and the hour of the coming of the Lord Jesus Christ.

After 2,600 years of desolation as a nation, Israel became a sovereign state in 1948, just as it is prophesied in Scripture. Ezekiel 38 says Israel will be at peace with its borders for a season. Then the nations from the north — Gog, Magog, Togarmah, Tubal and Meshech — will think an evil thought and they will invade Israel. The good news is, the Bible predicts the outcome of this confrontation: *Israel's enemies will be destroyed in one day!*

We are in a season of the time of the fulfillment of the prophecies regarding Israel and Jesus' return for His Church.

The cloud of witnesses are the saints spoken of in Hebrews, chapter 11, and our loved ones who have gone before us. We don't know how much the saints in heaven know of what is going on in the earth, but we do know they are interested, because they started the race which we are to finish.

It is time to lay aside everything that would hold us back or disqualify us and press ahead **"toward the goal for the prize of the upward call of God in Christ Jesus"** (Philippians 3:14).

What is holding you back from doing what God has called you to do? What is holding you back from reaching the people God has called you to reach? It is time to lay aside the weights, the excuses, and the procrastination and go with the vision God has placed in your heart.

We can no longer camp with "us four and no more." We must reach our cities, our nation, and other nations with the Good News of Jesus Christ.

God has given every person time, ability, and resources to make a difference in the earth. If you get your eyes off of Jesus and on materialism, you will be sidetracked. Sometimes people get in such a rat race with things to do, places to go, and people to see that they forget the real reason they are on the earth.

Jesus is the One we are to keep in focus. If men fail, we can keep going for Jesus. We're not to check out of the church, out of the Kingdom of God, or out of working for God just because someone else makes a mistake or gets off track.

Millions of lives are on the line, and we have an assignment to complete. It may not be in another nation or before large crowds. It may be with your next-door neighbor, or it may be working with a group of children, teens, or senior citizens.

This is not a time to quit, to be sidetracked, to point fingers at other people, or to find fault and excuse yourself from your call. The clock is ticking, and we are in the countdown to the end.

First Corinthians 14:3 AMP says:

But [on the other hand], the one who prophesies [who interprets the divine will and purpose in inspired preaching and teaching] speaks to men for their upbuilding and constructive spiritual progress and encouragement and consolation.

It is my intent to help you mature spiritually — through the prophetic word as well as through practical situations I have overcome with the application of God's Word — so you can enjoy "heaven on earth" now and impart to others the divine life you have received so we are ready for "takeoff" at Jesus' appearance!

A good place to start is to understand and then possess God's heartbeat.

For God so loved the world, that he gave his only begotten Son, that whosoever believeth in him should not period, but have everlasting life.

— John 3:16 KJV

2

POSSESSING GOD'S HEARTBEAT

God's heartbeat is "people." You don't have to read very far in the Bible to discover how much God loves people.

In Genesis 1, you can read about how God created the world, the sun, moon and stars, the planets, and then vegetation and animals, over which man was given the commission to "take dominion."

God said:

> "Let Us make man in Our image, according to Our likeness; let them have dominion over the fish of the sea, over the birds of the air, and over the cattle, over all the earth and over every creeping thing that creeps on the earth."
>
> So God created man in His own image; in the image of God He created him; male and female He created them.
>
> Then God blessed them, and God said to them, "Be fruitful and multiply; fill the earth and subdue it; have dominion over the fish of the sea, over the birds of the air, and over every living thing that moves on the earth."
>
> Then God saw everything that He had made, and indeed it was very good.
>
> **Genesis 1:26-28,31**

God made everything beautiful with one purpose in mind. It's the same purpose a builder has who builds houses, condominiums, townhouses, and apartments: He builds with *people* in mind.

Man was not an afterthought when God created planet earth. He had man in mind when He created the first star. When God formed the rivers and dug out the oceans, He was thinking about you and me. The balance of nature is a testimony of God's divine plan to put man in the earth to live in harmony and happiness.

When Adam and Eve failed, immediately God stepped in and said, "I'm going to crush the devil's head with the seed of a woman. The Messiah will be born through a virgin birth." (Genesis 3:15.) God was expressing His love for man, even though man had fallen.

All through the Old Testament, animal sacrifices were offered to atone for man's sin, which was a type and shadow of what was to come. God accepted the blood of animals as a covering for the sin of people so He could still have fellowship with them. He wasn't pleased with the animal sacrifices, but He was pleased that He could show mercy to get man back.

One day John the Baptist was at the Jordan River, and as he saw Jesus walking toward him, he said, **"Behold! The Lamb of God who takes away the sin of the world!"** (John 1:29).

God had provided Himself with a sacrifice. Abraham

foretold it when he offered up his son, Isaac, and called on God Who intervened and sent a ram to take Isaac's place. Abraham called His name *Jehovah-Jireh*, the God Who sees ahead and makes provision.

God saw ahead of our sin and made provision for a Savior. He sent His Son Jesus Christ, the Lamb of God, to take away the sin of the world.

Jesus Had a Heart for Sinners

In Matthew 9 Jesus chose Matthew, a tax collector, as one of His disciples. He said to Matthew, "Follow Me." Immediately, Matthew left his tax collecting business and followed Him. Jesus went to Matthew's house to have dinner. It was similar to His visit to Zacchaeus's house. Matthew was a well-known sinner, and he had a lot of friends who were sinners.

When was the last time you ate with an A-1 quality sinner?

As Jesus passed on from there, He saw a man named Matthew sitting at the tax office. And He said to him, "Follow Me." So he arose and followed Him.

Now it happened, as Jesus sat at the table in the house, that behold, many tax collectors and sinners came and sat down with Him and His disciples.

And when the Pharisees saw it, they said to His disciples, "Why does your Teacher eat with tax collectors and sinners?"

When Jesus heard that, He said to them, "Those who

are well have no need of a physician, but those who are sick.

"But go and learn what this means: 'I desire mercy and not sacrifice.' For I did not come to call the righteous, but sinners, to repentance."

Matthew 9:9-13

Jesus had a heart for sinners. Matthew 11:19 says that Jesus was known as "a friend of sinners." He was a friend of people who weren't religiously acceptable. If we're going to possess God's heartbeat, we must love these people, too.

Some people love God. It's just people they can't stand! But the second commandment is like the first, for the cross goes from upward to outward. **"You shall love your neighbor as yourself"** (Matthew 22:39). Jesus said the criteria for loving others is the way you love yourself.

Think of some of the people with whom Jesus spent time. Peter was the one who got off the boat on the Sea of Galilee to walk on the water, the one who went up on the Mount of Transfiguration.

The night Jesus was betrayed, He was grilled, mocked, and ridiculed, and Peter was approached as "one who knew that man." Peter denied Jesus. In fact, he denied Him three times. With the third denial, Peter cursed. I don't believe Peter got his language problem after the Last Supper! He had a problem controlling his tongue all along.

Some of the guys I worked with in the oil fields acted like they had taken a training course in cursing! They were real fluent. But, if you would cuss after spending three years with Jesus, as Peter did, you've got a real problem. The good news is, in spite of Peter's actions, Jesus chose him to preach the sermon on the Day of Pentecost.

James and John were called "the sons of thunder." They wanted to call fire from heaven and burn a village full of people who rejected Jesus. Sometimes we get such a warped idea of what the disciples were like. They were no different than people today.

Sin basically has never changed. People who lie and cuss today are just like the ones who lied and cussed 2,000 years ago. The people who are immoral today are like the people who sinned in centuries past.

Jesus said it wasn't the well who needed a physician but the sick. The person who isn't right with God in his heart is sick with a disease called "sin." There is disease in people's bodies. There also is dis-ease in people's minds when they are filled with torment, fear, anguish, and anxiety. When you can't be at peace with your family and in love with your children, with your mother, father, brothers, and sisters, there is dis-ease in your home.

Are your finances sick? Do you have more month than you have money to pay all the bills? Do you feel pain in your heart because of the lack?

It doesn't matter what level you have reached in

government, society, the marketplace, or the business world. If you don't have Jesus, you have needs in your life.

God's heart beats for people. In John 3:16, Jesus said, **"For God so loved the world that He gave His only begotten Son, that whoever believes in Him should not perish but have everlasting life."**

God's heart beats for those who are lost and for those who are down and out, as well as for those who are up and out.

There has to be a change in our hearts if we are going to reach this world for Jesus Christ. A lot of people could reach others if only they liked people. But their prejudice, bigotry, attitudes of indifference, and callousness are evident. Their actions and body language speak louder than their words.

God, deliver us from bigoted thoughts about other people regardless of their color or nationality. You can put an arm around all kinds of people and demonstrate God's love to them, in Jesus' name.

The Good Samaritan Loved People

Two men were walking from Jerusalem to Jericho. They saw a man lying at the side of the road, beaten by robbers, bleeding and dying. The two men, both religious, walked by and acted like they didn't see him.

In Matthew 9:13, Jesus said, **"I desire mercy and not sacrifice...."** Jesus hated the stinking sacrifices of men because they substituted them for God's mercy. They substituted religious tradition and went through the motions of religion so they wouldn't even see hurting people.

Jesus wants to reach people who are messed up and hurting. He made a way to reach them through His shed blood.

Are the people in the nursing homes, in Russia, Haiti, Nepal, or Zaire not there just because we don't see them? How about the teenagers on our streets? Thank God for people who are lifting up their eyes, looking on the fields, and allowing the compassion of Christ to move them toward those who are hurting.

A Samaritan, despised by the Jews, came by and saw the wounded man. The Bible says he went to him and began to pour oil into his wounds, put him on his donkey, carried him to an inn, paid the innkeeper, and essentially said, "If it costs more, I'll pay it." Jesus asked, "Which man was the neighbor who demonstrated My love?"

God's Heartbeat Is Lifting People

I'm glad Jesus left heaven and came to this earth, because He saw us bleeding and dying on the Jericho road. He was the Good Samaritan, not just going to do religious things. The world has religion, and people go through motions and rituals, but that's not what Jesus is after. He loves people.

In one of our monthly government-subsidized apartment crusades, our children's pastor brought the boys and girls who were going to go on a short-term missions trip to share the love of God with hurting people. He said, "Before you go overseas, you need to go across town."

Before the crusade, the children's pastor instructed the children, "When you knock on doors to invite people to the crusade, you may have to wash the dishes and clean up the apartment if the parents won't let the children come."

One of our young boys knocked on a door where several kids were hanging out an upstairs window. The dad said, "They have already been invited and they can't come. They've got to clean up the kitchen, wash the dishes, and clean the floor." The young boy from Victory said, "We will do it." He went and got his buddies, and they began to clean the floors and wash the dishes.

Then the father said, "I guess I'll have to let them go now. I need some free time anyway." They brought those little children into the tent for the children's service, and all of them received Christ on Friday night while Dad was sitting in the apartment all by himself.

When we arrived at the apartment complex on Saturday, I did what everyone else was doing. I knocked on doors and invited people to come to the crusade and to accept Jesus Christ.

I walked up to a car that was jump-starting another car, stuck my head in and said, "Are you going to come hear me preach?" There are different ways to catch fish. Sometimes you are very quiet. At other times, you just jump in!

He said, "No, no, I ain't coming. I've got to keep all these kids." He was sitting there, patting the accelerator and drinking his alcohol. I felt the love of God for this man, so I said, "Where's Mamma?" He said, "She ran off a year and a half ago."

My heart really went out to this man. I said, "Let me pray for you." When I started to pray for him, the Holy Ghost came all over him and he accepted Jesus Christ right there.

After the crusade, our children's pastor told me the story of what the kids had done the night before. Their love opened the hearts of an entire family.

When you share love, it comes back to you. When you share your life, you will find it. Jesus said, **"For whoever desires to save his life will lose it, but whoever loses his life for My sake will find it"** (Matthew 16:25).

Is Your Life People-Centered?

Some people don't wake up spiritually until they are sixty years old and their whole life is nearly gone. They have spent it making a living, raising their kids and getting a degree, yet they have never discovered what life is all about. They are empty on the inside.

If God's heart is beating in your heart, you will find a way to reach people on a regular basis. *The heart of a soulwinner is the heart of God.*

All over the world, people are waiting for those who

will hear the heartbeat of God, who will sell their lives out to Him and say, "I'll go where You want me to go. I'll do what You want me to do. I'm fed up with living an empty life, just living for myself and for things."

At twenty years of age, it was this revelation that changed my life. I have never regretted giving my life for people. You may say, "But I'm not a preacher." You can still love people and touch them. *Every day* there are opportunities to touch hurting people.

Jonah Refused To Touch the People of Nineveh

God loved the people of Nineveh, although it was a wicked city, full of the devil, all types of idolatry, and slaughter of children.

God spoke to Jonah, who lived in Israel, "Go, preach to the people of Nineveh." Jonah didn't want to go. He knew what those people did to their enemies. The Israelites hated the Ninevites because of their godlessness and ruthless war practices. So Jonah turned and went the other way.

Jonah got on one of those Mediterranean cruise boats and a storm hit. The men cast lots, trying to figure out who was causing the problem. Jonah knew it was him, so he finally fessed up and said, "Boys, if you'll throw me overboard, the storm will stop." They pitched him overboard.

Jonah spent three days and three nights in a prayer

retreat in the lower Mediterranean, shut in alone with God. (God had prepared a fish to swallow him.) After he and the Lord had a face-to-face talk, Jonah said, "I'll go to Nineveh, Lord." The fish spit Jonah out, and when Jonah hit the ground, he headed to Nineveh!

When he got there, he said, **"Yet forty days, and Nineveh shall be overthrown!"** (Jonah 3:4). Jonah missed the purpose of this message, but the Ninevites heard it the way God intended.

Jonah went out underneath a tree to sit and wait for the destruction of Nineveh. I believe his thoughts went something like this: "God is going to roast and toast them all!" He had visions of Sodom and Gomorrah all over again, thinking about Elijah calling fire down from heaven. But inside of that city, a king bowed his head in a spirit of repentance, then rose up and published a decree:

> **Let neither man nor beast, herd nor flock, taste anything; do not let them eat, or drink water.**
>
> **But let man and beast be covered with sackcloth, and cry mightily to God; yes, let every one turn from his evil way and from the violence that is in his hands.**
>
> **Who can tell if God will turn and relent, and turn away from His fierce anger, so that we may not perish?**
>
> **Jonah 3:7-9**

When people are repentant, God will change judgment. That is His nature. The whole town — 120,000 people — fasted and prayed and repented before God.

Meanwhile, Jonah sat and waited for judgment to fall. He didn't know about the repentance, fasting, and prayer.

A worm started eating away on the plant that gave Jonah shade until it was gone. Then a hot east wind rolled across the desert and the sun beat down. Sitting in that heat, Jonah was mad at God for not destroying the people of Nineveh.

In the last two verses of the book of Jonah, God had a little talk with him:

> **"You have had pity on the plant for which you have not labored, nor made it grow, which came up in a night and perished in a night.**
>
> **"And should I not pity Nineveh, that great city, in which are more than one hundred and twenty thousand persons who cannot discern between their right hand and their left — and much livestock?"**
>
> **Jonah 4:10,11**

It is time to move out of selfishness into God's vision for the world. God's heartbeat, in a nutshell, is that we love Him with all of our hearts, then take His life and love to others, from one corner of the earth to the other!

3

ABLAZE WITH GOD'S SPIRIT

by Sharon Daugherty

The Church of this hour, God's last-day Church, will arise and shine with the glory of the Lord, causing His glory to be seen in all the earth, just as Isaiah prophesied.

When we speak of the Church, we are speaking of the individual believers who make up the entire Body of Christ. With this in mind, let's read the prophecy from Isaiah 60:1-5:

> Arise, shine; for your light has come! And the glory of the Lord is risen upon you.
>
> For behold, the darkness shall cover the earth, and deep darkness the people; but the Lord will arise over you, and His glory will be seen upon you.
>
> The Gentiles shall come to your light, and kings to the brightness of your rising.
>
> Lift up your eyes all around, and see: they all gather together, they come to you; your sons shall come from afar, and your daughters shall be nursed at your side.
>
> Then you shall see and become radiant, and your heart shall swell with joy; because the abundance of the

**sea shall be turned to you, the wealth of the Gentiles shall
come to you.**

This isn't a picture of wimpy warriors. It is a picture
of mighty warriors, radiant with the character of God
and ablaze with His Spirit – a people who are recipients
of the wealth of the wicked (Proverbs 13:22) that they
might be about the Father's business, unhindered in the
financial realm.

God promised to pour out His Spirit upon *all flesh* in
the last days. Let's look at this account from Joel 2:28-30:

**And it shall come to pass afterward that I will pour
out My Spirit on all flesh; your sons and your daughters
shall prophesy, your old men shall dream dreams, your
young men shall see visions.**

**And also on My menservants and on My maid-
servants I will pour out My Spirit in those days.**

**And I will show wonders in the heavens and in the
earth....**

I was invited to speak at a women's retreat in a
denominational church in our city that usually doesn't
allow women to teach from the pulpit.

In this setting, the women asked me how I felt about
women teaching the Word. I said, "I didn't come to change
your doctrines. I came because you invited me to share by
the Spirit of God."

They insisted, "But we want to know." They quoted
every scripture that has anything to say about women of
the Bible before I could get them out of my mouth. I

attempted to bring the whole counsel of God's Word together, from both the Old and New Testaments.

One of the ladies said, "There is one scripture I have held onto, and that is Joel 2:28, where God says in the last days He will pour out His Spirit upon all flesh — not only on the men, but on the women and children, too."

In Acts 2:17-21, in referring to the baptism of the Holy Spirit, Peter quoted Joel's prophecy. He said of the 120 in the Upper Room:

> **For these are not drunk, as you suppose, since it is only the third hour of the day.**
>
> **But this is what was spoken by the prophet Joel.**
>
> **Acts 2:15,16**

Peter explained that the people (both men and women) were filled with new wine — the wine of God's Spirit — which is not a natural drink, but a spiritual drink. When they drank of the Spirit, it made them bold and courageous for Jesus Christ. It made them want to go and do the works of Jesus.

This is exactly what the pouring out of God's Spirit will do for us in our lives in these last days. As we are empowered with the Spirit, we will do the works of Jesus. We will be mighty warriors for the Kingdom of God, sharing Him with others.

4

PERILS OF THE LAST-DAY CHURCH

by Sharon Daugherty

I want to bring you the other side of the coin — the perils or dangers of the last-day Church that will confront us.

In meditating upon all the good things that will happen in the last hour of the Church age, we tend to forget the perils that will take place. As mighty men and women of the last-day Church, we need to maintain a proper balance by looking at both sides of the coin.

Paul clearly presented some of these perils in 2 Timothy 3:1-7 KJV:

> **This know also, that in the last days perilous times shall come.**
>
> **For men shall be lovers of their own selves, covetous, boasters, proud, blasphemers, disobedient to parents, unthankful, unholy,**
>
> **Without natural affection, trucebreakers, false accusers, incontinent, fierce, despisers of those that are good,**
>
> **Traitors, heady, highminded, lovers of pleasures more than lovers of God;**

> **Having a form of godliness, but denying the power thereof: from such turn away.**
>
> **For of this sort are they which creep into houses, and lead captive silly women laden with sins, led away with divers lusts,**
>
> **Ever learning, and never able to come to the knowledge of the truth.**

Let's look briefly at each of these perils that Paul mentions so we will be alert to give them *no place* in our lives.

Lovers of Self

Paul was saying, "People will be selfish and self-centered."

I don't know if you have noticed, but today we have weight loss centers, body building centers, and every kind of cosmetology you can think of to help us look young, stay young, look thin, and keep our hair from turning gray! A hundred years ago, such centers never existed. They keep our focus on ourselves.

Many books on improving self-image are available. Sometimes people go through difficult times in their lives, but the thing that will build their self-image more than anything else is when they learn their true identity in Jesus Christ. You can read every book that has ever been written on self-image, but if you don't get into THE BOOK (the Bible), you will always be insecure and motivated by fear. It's time to identify with this Book, because it will take care of every need you will ever have, and it will bring you into the right balance in your life.

Covetous

The Greek word for *covetous* is *epithumeo*. *Epi* means "intensively" and *thumeo* means "with passion." In other words, *covetous* in the Greek means "to fix your desire on something intensively and with passion, whether it's a good thing or a bad thing, to long for it and lust after it so much that you are determined to get it at any cost."

There are examples of covetousness in the Bible, and it still exists in our society today. Let's look at two biblical examples of covetousness — one from the Old Testament and one from the New.

Ahab's Covetousness

Ahab wanted Naboth's vineyard, which was located close to Ahab's living quarters. Ahab wanted it enough that he began pouting about it after Naboth refused to give it up. Then Jezebel came on the scene.

Jezebel was as wicked as she could be. Basically, she said to Ahab, "What are you doing? You are the king of this whole land. You can take what you want." Then she promised to get it for him. She had Naboth killed. Covetousness will drive you to any length to get what you want.

Elijah the prophet showed up because God would not let Ahab get away with this kind of behavior.

The Spirit of God spoke to Elijah in 1 Kings 21:17-23:

> **Then the word of the Lord came to Elijah the Tishbite, saying,**
>
> **"Arise, go down to meet Ahab king of Israel, who lives in Samaria. There he is, in the vineyard of Naboth, where he has gone down to take possession of it.**
>
> **"You shall speak to him, saying, 'Thus says the Lord: "Have you murdered and also taken possession?"' And you shall speak to him, saying, 'Thus says the Lord: "In the place where dogs licked the blood of Naboth, dogs shall lick your blood, even yours."'"**
>
> **So Ahab said to Elijah, "Have you found me, O my enemy?" And he answered, "I have found you, because you have sold yourself to do evil in the sight of the Lord:**
>
> **"'Behold, I will bring calamity on you. I will take away your posterity, and will cut off from Ahab every male in Israel, both bond and free.**
>
> **"'I will make your house like the house of Jeroboam the son of Nebat, and like the house of Baasha the son of Ahijah, because of the provocation with which you have provoked Me to anger, and made Israel sin.'**
>
> **"And concerning Jezebel the Lord also spoke, saying, 'The dogs shall eat Jezebel by the wall of Jezreel.'"**

Jezebel was eaten by the dogs just as Elijah had said, because she didn't repent. God's mercy was extended toward Ahab, however, because he humbled himself after hearing Elijah's prophecy. The judgment did fall on Ahab's son.

The Covetousness of Ananias and Sapphira

In Acts, chapter 5, we see a New Testament example of covetousness in Ananias and Sapphira. Covetousness over money they had promised to God caused them to lie to the Holy Ghost.

> **And he [Ananias] kept back part of the proceeds, his wife also being aware of it, and brought a certain part and laid it at the apostles' feet.**
>
> **But Peter said, "Ananias, why has Satan filled your heart to lie to the Holy Spirit and keep back part of the price of the land for yourself?**
>
> **"While it remained, was it not your own? And after it was sold, was it not in your own control? Why have you conceived this thing in your heart? You have not lied to men but to God."**
>
> **Acts 5:2-4**

Ananias and Sapphira didn't have to commit to give all of their proceeds to God. If, in the very beginning, they had said, "We are going to give a certain portion," then they would not have put themselves in a position to lie. But they had made a covenant that they were going to give *all* of the proceeds. Peter, through knowledge the Holy Spirit gave him, knew that Ananias had lied.

> **Then Ananias, hearing these words, fell down and breathed his last. So great fear came upon all those who heard these things.**

27

And the young men arose and wrapped him up, carried him out, and buried him.

Now it was about three hours later when his wife came in, not knowing what had happened.

And Peter answered her, "Tell me whether you sold the land for so much?" She said, "Yes, for so much."

Then Peter said to her, "How is it that you have agreed together to test the Spirit of the Lord? Look, the feet of those who have buried your husband are at the door, and they will carry you out."

Then immediately she fell down at his feet and breathed her last. And the young men came in and found her dead, and carrying her out, buried her by her husband.

So great fear came upon all the church and upon all who heard these things.

Acts 5:5-11

The lives of Ahab, Ananias, and Sapphira are examples of what happens when a spirit of covetousness takes hold of a person.

Sometimes people start out with a right heart motive and later compromise and get off track. Billy Joe and I have seen people go through bankruptcy and other terrible troubles because of going back on their word, not just to men, but to God.

Love of Money – A Driving Force to Covetousness

Covetousness can creep in upon a person because of a love of money. First Timothy 6:10 says, **"For the *love of*** *money* **is a root of all kinds of evil, for which some have strayed from the faith in their greediness, and pierced themselves through with many sorrows."** The love of money will drive you to accumulate more "things."

Right Money Motives

Some people have a motive to get wealth to put into God's Kingdom. Years ago, we met such a man in Pennsylvania when we were traveling in ministry. We met him at a Christian Retreat where we ministered and served as pastor of the grounds for one summer.

Chris and his wife, who were from Switzerland, couldn't speak any English. They came to America in the early 50s and began to work in a plant nursery. As they worked, they learned more of the language, and God began to bless them.

Chris went to a tent meeting in the early 60s where Oral Roberts shared his vision to build a university. Brother Roberts asked the people who were willing to do so to make a financial commitment to the ministry.

Chris and his wife shared their testimony with us. "We didn't have that much to give, but we felt God wanted us to enter into that commitment."

The same week they made their commitment to Oral Roberts' Ministry, they received a job raise. They continued to receive raises in their work in the nursery. The day came when the nursery owner's son declined the offer from his father to take over the nursery business.

The son had attended college and majored in horti-culture. But when it was time for the father to turn the entire business over to him, the son said, "Chris is the one who should own and run this place."

The nursery was turned over to Chris. It became the largest nursery in the state of New Jersey, serving people in other states as well.

God blessed Chris and his wife, and the day came when they were able to accumulate enough money to buy 500 acres in Pennsylvania to establish Blue Mountain Christian Retreat, fulfilling a dream that God had put in their hearts. Putting God first in everything, they built a Christian Retreat for families and ministers to come for meetings and rest. To this day, it is a beautiful Christian Retreat in the Blue Mountains of Pennsylvania. God has continued to bless Chris and his family.

God will bless people today, too, whose motives are pure before Him.

Boasters (Proud)

Paul said that in the last days, before Jesus' return for His Church, men would be boasters (proud).

In Acts, chapter 12, King Herod put Peter in jail. He planned to behead him, just like he had beheaded James. However, Acts 12:5 says, **"Constant prayer was offered to God for him** [Peter] **by the church."** As a result of prayer, an angel brought deliverance to Peter, intercepting the prideful plans of King Herod (vv. 7-18). King Herod was so upset about Peter's escape that he had the prison guard killed.

A group of men from Tyre and Sidon who wanted to stay in good relationship with King Herod came to him. Herod financially supported their area of the country, so they didn't want to be on the outs with him.

> **Now Herod had been very angry with the people of Tyre and Sidon; but they came to him with one accord, and having made Blastus the king's personal aide their friend, they asked for peace, because their country was supplied with food by the king's country.**
>
> **So on a set day Herod, arrayed in royal apparel, sat on his throne and gave an oration to them.**
>
> **And the people kept shouting, "The voice of a god and not of a man!"**
>
> **Acts 12:20-22**

Herod loved the accolades of men. The Bible says he was boastful and proud and took all the glory to himself. As a result, when the people called him a god and not a man, scripture says, **"Immediately an angel of the Lord struck him, because he did not give glory to God. And *he was eaten by worms and died"*** (Acts 12:23). This judgment happened in the New Testament!

It is time to stop the boasting and pride. A boaster is someone who brags on himself and sneers at God. He is self-sufficient.

Boasting and pride will lead to destruction. **"Pride goes before destruction, and a haughty spirit before a fall"** (Proverbs 16:18).

Blasphemers

Blasphemers are those who defame, rail, injure, or speak evil of those who stand for God.

Second Peter 3:3,4 says:

> **Knowing this first: that scoffers will come in the last days, walking according to their own lusts,**
>
> **And saying, "Where is the promise of His coming? For since the fathers fell asleep, all things continue as they were from the beginning of creation."**

Some people are scoffing at the things of God in this hour. When you talk about "Jesus is coming soon," they scoff and say, "Sure, He's coming soon. They said that in 1940, and He still hasn't come."

These people are headed for trouble. They are scoffers and blasphemers of the Church, the things the Church stands for, God's ministers, and His people.

Disobedient to Parents

Second Timothy 3:2 says that in the last days there will be those who are **"disobedient to parents."** They won't respect authority, and they won't do what they are told to do. Instead, they will do what they *want* to do.

32

In Ephesians 6:1-3, Paul said:

> **Children, obey your parents in the Lord, for this is right.**

> **"Honor your father and mother," which is the first commandment with promise:**

> **"That it may be well with you and you may live long on the earth."**

Paul was saying that children who are disobedient to their parents and who mock their parents are playing with life and death. When you disobey, you forfeit the promise of Ephesians 6:3 *that it will be well with you and that you will live a long life.*

Unthankful

Paul said that in the last days there would be those who are unthankful. They won't express gratitude when something is done to help them or bless them. Instead, they "expect" things to be done for them. When you go to a country that doesn't have much, we have found that the people are usually grateful for everything.

Unholy

Paul said that in the last days there would be those who are unholy, unclean, immoral, and living with no restraint.

Second Timothy 2:19 says, **"...Let everyone who names the name of Christ depart from iniquity."** That means *leave it.* If you name Jesus as your Lord, then leave sin. Walk away from it. Separate yourself from it. If you are naming the name of Christ, yet you are living like the devil, you are a hypocrite.

Obviously, every person falls short at times, because no one is perfect. But, we are to make an effort to follow after Jesus Christ with all of our hearts so we never intentionally sin.

First John 3:6-8 says:

> **Whoever abides in Him does not sin. Whoever sins has neither seen Him nor known Him.**
>
> **Little children, let no one deceive you. He who practices righteousness is righteous, just as He is righteous.**
>
> **He who sins is of the devil, for the devil has sinned from the beginning....**

The person who continues to walk in sin when he knows he shouldn't lusts after sin. This person has given himself over to the lust of the flesh, and he doesn't want to get out of it. In such a case, God says, "They are of the devil."

Proverbs 6:27 says, **"Can a man take fire in his bosom, and his clothes not be burned?"** In other words, when you play with sin, it will burn you. Scripture says that sin has pleasure, but only for a season (Hebrews 11:25). Give it a little time and it will destroy your life. That's exactly what Satan intends for it to do.

Satan hates every person on the earth, even those who worship him. They may think he likes them, because he gives them power for a season. Then he kills them. It is because we are created in God's image that Satan is out to destroy us. We can only stand secure as we walk in obedience and faith in Jesus.

Without Natural Affection

In the last days, there will be those who are **"without natural affection"** (2 Timothy 3:3 KJV). Paul is talking about homosexuality, lesbianism, incest, and every kind of sexual perversion you can think of.

Romans 1:18-32 in the *Amplified Bible* expounds on "unnatural affection":

> For God's [holy] wrath and indignation are revealed from heaven against all ungodliness and unrighteousness of men, who in their wickedness repress and hinder the truth and make it inoperative.
>
> For that which is known about God is evident to them and made plain in their inner consciousness, because God [Himself] has shown it to them.
>
> For ever since the creation of the world His invisible nature and attributes, that is, His eternal power and divinity, have been made intelligible and clearly discernible in and through the things that have been made (His handiworks). So [men] are without excuse [altogether without any defense or justification],
>
> Because when they knew and recognized Him as God, they did not honor and glorify Him as God or give Him thanks. But instead they became futile and godless in their thinking [with vain imaginings, foolish reasoning, and

stupid speculations] and their senseless minds were darkened.

Claiming to be wise, they became fools [professing to be smart, they made simpletons of themselves].

And by them the glory and majesty and excellence of the immortal God were exchanged for and represented by images, resembling mortal man and birds and beasts and reptiles.

Therefore God gave them up in the lusts of their [own] hearts to sexual impurity, to the dishonoring of their bodies among themselves [abandoning them to the degrading power of sin],

Because they exchanged the truth of God for a lie and worshiped and served the creature rather than the Creator, Who is blessed forever! Amen (so be it).

For this reason God gave them over and abandoned them to vile affections and degrading passions. For their women exchanged their natural function for an unnatural and abnormal one,

And the men also turned from natural relations with women and were set ablaze (burning out, consumed) with lust for one another — men committing shameful acts with men and suffering in their own bodies and personalities the inevitable consequences and penalty of their wrongdoing and going astray, which was [their] fitting retribution.

And so, since they did not see fit to acknowledge God or approve of Him or consider Him worth the knowing, God gave them over to a base and condemned mind to do things not proper or decent but loathsome,

Until they were filled (permeated and saturated) with every kind of unrighteousness, iniquity, grasping and covetous greed, and malice. [They were] full of envy and jealousy, murder, strife, deceit and treachery, ill will and cruel ways. [They were] secret backbiters and gossipers,

Slanderers, hateful to and hating God, full of insolence, arrogance, [and] boasting; inventors of new forms of evil, disobedient and undutiful to parents.

[They were] without understanding, conscienceless and faithless, heartless and loveless [and] merciless.

Though they are fully aware of God's righteous decree that those who do such things deserve to die, they not only do them themselves but approve and applaud others who practice them.

Now, let's look at verses 26-32 in *The Living Bible*:

That is why God let go of them and let them do all these evil things, so that even their women turned against God's natural plan for them and indulged in sex sin with each other.

And the men, instead of having a normal sex relationship with women, burned with lust for each other, men doing shameful things with other men and, as a result, getting paid within their own souls with the penalty they so richly deserved.

So it was that when they gave God up and would not even acknowledge him, God gave them up to doing everything their evil minds could think of.

Their lives became full of every kind of wickedness and sin, of greed and hate, envy, murder, fighting, lying, bitterness, and gossip.

>They were backbiters, haters of God, insolent, proud braggarts, always thinking of new ways of sinning and continually being disobedient to their parents.

>They tried to misunderstand, broke their promises, and were heartless — without pity.

>They were fully aware of God's death penalty for these crimes, yet they went right ahead and did them anyway, and encouraged others to do them, too.

God, in His loving mercy, has given us time to repent. He doesn't want us to destroy ourselves, and neither does He want us to be destroyed. But if we go on in stubbornness and disobedience, we will bring God's judgment upon ourselves.

Let's examine what Paul said in Romans 2:4-8 TLB:

>Don't you realize how patient he is being with you? Or don't you care? *Can't you see that he has been waiting all this time without punishing you, to give you time to turn from your sin?* His kindness is meant to lead you to repentance.

>But no, you won't listen; and so you are saving up terrible punishment for yourselves because of your stubbornness in refusing to turn from your sin; for there is going to come a day of wrath when God will be the just Judge of all the world.

>He will give each one whatever his deeds deserve.

>He will give eternal life to those who patiently do the will of God, seeking for the unseen glory and honor and eternal life that he offers.

>But he will terribly punish those who fight against

the truth of God and walk in evil ways — God's anger will be poured out upon them.

In America, we have laws, and if people disobey them, they can end up in prison. God has laws, and He has a prison, too. That prison is *hell*. He doesn't want us to go to hell. It's not His desire that any man perish, but that everyone would have the opportunity to receive eternal life. He leaves the choice up to us to obey, and because of His goodness, He has given us time to repent.

Trucebreakers

In the last days, there will be trucebreakers — people who don't keep their word. They will say one thing, but because of no self-discipline, no ability to be faithful, they will break the truce (or covenant).

We see this happening today in marriages and in business situations. God is saying, "Keep your word."

False Accusers

False accusers are those who falsely accuse, who tell lies and slander people. Revelation 12:10 calls the devil **"the accuser of our brethren."** The Greek word for *accuser* is *diabolos*.

A false accuser is someone who finds fault with a person or the conduct of someone, then spreads his opinions and criticisms about that person.

Normally, the false accuser is someone who is out to destroy rather than to help. They want to tell something about someone else, not so that person can be changed, but so they can cause division. Simply stated, a false accuser *is out to destroy and divide.*

The person who really cares for someone and sees that he is in sin, will go to that person and confront him. That's what the Bible says we are supposed to do. They will try to rectify the situation. If that doesn't work, they will go to the elders of the church with the situation. They will try their best to reconcile the situation. (See Matthew 18:15-17.)

Incontinent

In the last days, there will be those who are incontinent. That means without self-control and self-restraint and consumed with lust. They are always seeking to gratify their flesh. They never think about the best of other people.

We have seen people who wanted someone else's spouse so bad they were willing to go to any extreme to get that person, even to the point of breaking up a marriage. They ruined other people's lives and thought only of themselves.

Fierce

There will be those who are fierce, which means "mean."

I read an article in a *Concerned Women for America Magazine*. One of the C.W.A. representatives attended a National Education Association meeting.

At this meeting, Planned Parenthood had signs advertising the teaching of sex to teenagers in the public schools and how to get free condoms so teenagers could practice "safe sex." (The only "safe sex" that exists is not having sex outside of the confines of marriage.) The abortionists were screaming their rights. The gays wanted people to take on their ideology, teaching homosexuality in the schools.

As the C.W.A. representative viewed the demonstrations, she said that many of the demonstrators were just plain "mean." This is a sign of the last days.

Despisers of Those Who Are Good

Another sign of the times we are in is that there are those who despise the people who are doing good. They hate anything and anyone promoting holiness.

Traitors

Traitors are those who say they are one of you, then they turn and betray you. There are traitors who have wormed their way into the church. They try to catch hold of something so they can take it to the world.

Then there are those who are traitors to the cross. They have never surrendered their lives to Jesus Christ. When I say *surrendered*, I mean "absolute surrender." I don't mean going through a confessional prayer and mentally assenting to the gospel when it's popular. I'm talking about someone who is willing to lay down his life, absolutely surrendered to Jesus Christ. We must be fully surrendered in the days we are living in, willing to take the heat, to be strong and zealous for God regardless of what is going on around us.

We aren't to be ashamed that we are Spirit-filled Christians, that we believe in healing, miracles and the gifts of the Spirit, and that we believe Jesus Christ is the same yesterday, today, and forever.

There Will Be a Falling Away

Second Thessalonians 2:1-4 says that in the last days, there will be a falling away:

> **Now, brethren, concerning the coming of our Lord Jesus Christ and our gathering together to Him, we ask you,**
>
> **Not to be soon shaken in mind or troubled, either by spirit or by word or by letter, as if from us, as though the day of Christ had come.**
>
> **Let no one deceive you by any means; for that Day will not come unless the falling away comes first, and the man of sin is revealed, the son of perdition,**
>
> **Who opposes and exalts himself above all that is called God or that is worshiped, so that he sits as God in the temple of God, showing himself that he is God.**

Several years ago as I was meditating upon this scripture, it was difficult for me to envision a falling away among the people that I knew. The sad thing is, it is now happening, not only in our own local Body, but in the Body of Christ as a whole.

I know people who were serving in the church, giving

of their time and doing the things they were supposed to be doing. They believed in the Bible, believed the things that were preached, and then allowed themselves to get out of the Word and out of prayer, to miss church, and to stop serving God.

They pulled back and said, "We're going to get out of all our obligations because we feel like we need to draw apart for a little while." I've seen them grow cold, like a coal pulled from a fire. When you heap a bunch of coals together, they will burn bright, but you pull those coals apart, and they will die out.

I've seen it in people's lives, spiritually speaking, and God is saying, "Turn back to your first love. Receive again the zeal for My Son. Go back to your roots. Go back to the time when you felt My presence in such a rich way you enjoyed coming to church, you loved the Word and you loved prayer."

Time keeps ticking away, and you don't know what tomorrow holds. You are playing with fire, yet God is calling you back into relationship with Him.

Heady/Highminded

There will be those who are heady, which means hotheaded or headstrong. There are a few people like this in the Body of Christ! You try to tell them something, and they say, "Bless God. Nobody tells me what to do. I'm submitted to God, not to man."

Then they want to prophesy their opinions to you of what they think you ought to be doing. If they're not submitted to and flowing under the leadership of a local Body, don't listen to them.

It's easy for them to say they submit to God, because they can't see Him. They make up in their minds what they think God said to them. Then they say, "This is what God told me to do." But a person who is submitted to God is willing to submit to God-ordained authority. Ephesians 5:21 says, **"Submitting to one another in the fear of God."**

Lovers of Pleasure
Rather Than Lovers of God

In our country, we've got every kind of entertainment you can think of: videos; swimming; snow skiing; sky-diving; horseback riding; hunting; and fishing. We've got helicopter rides, restaurants of every kind, and all kinds of competitive sports. People pay big money for entertainment and to fly to and from where the action is. Paul said that in the last days, men would be **"lovers of pleasure rather than lovers of God"** (2 Timothy 3:4).

God is not against a time of rest, recreation, and relaxation, but for some people, it is on their minds all the time. As soon as Friday work is over, they hook their boat to their car or truck and head for the lake, never giving a thought about worshipping God.

Having a Form of Godliness
but Denying the Power Thereof

There are people who have a form of religion, but they aren't flowing in the power of the Holy Spirit and doing the works of Jesus — healing the sick, seeing people delivered from drugs, alcohol, and demonic possession. Paul is saying, "There will be those who carry a form of godliness, but they won't have any power." Scripture says, **"...from such turn away"** (2 Timothy 3:5 KJV).

Paul goes on, **"For of this sort are they which creep into houses, and lead captive silly women laden with sins, led away with divers lusts"** (2 Timothy 3:6 KJV).

If you, as a woman, are in a relationship where your husband is not seeking God, oftentimes there is an opportunity for you to be "taken in" by different teachings, running here and there. You need to stay within a Body where you are nurtured spiritually, where you can be protected from people who might, as this scripture says, creep in and lead you away with divers lusts.

Ever learning, and never able to come to the knowledge of the truth.

Now as Jannes and Jambres withstood Moses, so do these also resist the truth: men of corrupt minds, reprobate concerning the faith.

2 Timothy 3:7,8 KJV

Jannes and Jambres were children of Israel in the wilderness, and God had set Moses as the leader. Jannes and Jambres resisted Moses. They basically said, "We're not going to follow you anymore. You go up to that mountain, and you are away from us for days. We are ready to have some action."

Jannes and Jambres took it upon themselves to lead a bunch of the people, pull them away from Moses and divide the group. Scripture says of these two men that they were **"...men of corrupt minds, reprobate concerning the faith"** (v. 8). The reward for their strife was death, and it is doubtful that they went to heaven.

Paul continues:

> **But they shall proceed no further: for their folly shall be manifest unto all men, as theirs also was.**
>
> **But thou hast fully known my doctrine, manner of life, purpose, faith, longsuffering, charity, patience,**
>
> **Persecutions, afflictions, which came unto me at Antioch, at Iconium, at Lystra; what persecutions I endured: but out of them all the Lord delivered me.**
>
> **Yea, and all that will live godly in Christ Jesus shall suffer persecution.**
>
> **But evil men and seducers shall wax worse and worse, deceiving, and being deceived.**
>
> **2 Timothy 3:9-13 KJV**

This is talking about the days we are living in right now. Then Paul gives advice as to what we must do in order to *not* be taken in by the traps and deceits of the enemy.

> But continue thou in the things which thou hast learned and hast been assured of, knowing of whom thou hast learned them;
>
> And that from a child thou hast known the holy scriptures, which are able to make thee wise unto salvation through faith which is in Christ Jesus.
>
> All scripture is given by inspiration of God, and is profitable for doctrine, for reproof, for correction, for instruction in righteousness.
>
> **2 Timothy 3:14-16 KJV**

If you will let the Word abide in you and if you will abide in the Word, it will reprove or correct you. It will tell you when you are wrong, and it will expose the very thoughts and intents of your heart. It will discern your soul from your spirit. Sometimes your soul tells you things and you may think it's your spirit. God doesn't want you to be led by your soulish realm, which is your mind, will, emotions, and intellect.

Instead, *let the Spirit lead you.* Your spirit can lead you when you read the Word on a daily basis, memorize it and meditate on it. The Word will help you to discern what is God and what comes from your own emotions, feelings, or thoughts.

Paul said the Word is for instruction in righteousness. When you are born again, you receive the righteousness of God in Christ, but there is a working out of your salvation that must yet take place. Note, I did not say to work to be saved. Salvation is received by faith because of the grace

47

of Jesus Christ. However, there are good works that He leads us to walk in after we are saved.

Philippians 2:12,13 says:

> **Work out your own salvation with fear and trembling;**
>
> **For it is God who works in you both to will and to do for His good pleasure.**

Some people stop short of "working out their own salvation." They don't get in the Word and allow themselves to be corrected or reproved.

James 1:25 says you can look in the perfect law of liberty (the Word of God), which is like a mirror. When you look in that mirror, it will reveal things to you.

The Bible says you can either remember what you saw in the mirror, or you can forget it. There are believers who are reading their Bibles every day, but they are forgetting what they read. As they walk through the day, anger, impatience, worry, and a lack of self-control dominate them rather than love, joy, and peace. If they don't remember what they saw in the mirror of the Word, they will be deceived.

Some believers are deceiving themselves. They are into a habit of reading their Bibles, but it is not evident in their lives. God is saying, "When you look into that law of liberty — that mirror of the Word — don't forget what you saw."

Then throughout the day when there are opportunities

for anger or for doing something wrong, the Holy Spirit will bring to your remembrance the things Jesus said. Paul says the Word is **"for instruction in righteousness** (or right living)**: that the man of God may be perfect, thoroughly furnished unto all good works"** (2 Timothy 3:16,17 KJV).

Perfect, as used in this verse, means "mature or complete." God wants us to mature. He doesn't want us to stay babies. The only way we can mature is through His Word.

5

COVETOUS OR CONTENT?

To impact the world with the Good News of Jesus Christ, we must be pure, holy vessels.

Covetousness, which Sharon taught on briefly in the previous chapter, is one of the primary reasons people get off course in their walk with God. It is the result of a lack of faith and trust in God. A covetous person has no confidence that God will take care of him or that He will supply for him. Therefore, he utilizes his own unholy drive and desire to obtain "things." The problem with it is that there is never enough, because nothing can take the place of faith in God.

Paul had much to say about being content rather than covetous.

> Not that I speak in regard to need, for I have learned in whatever state I am, to be content:
>
> I know how to be abased, and I know how to abound. Everywhere and in all things I have learned both to be full and to be hungry, both to abound and to suffer need.
>
> I can do all things through Christ who strengthens me.
>
> **Philippians 4:11-13**

Paul was saying, "There are places I am called where there is abundance, and there are places I am called where there is lack, but I have learned not to be moved by the circumstances. I am content, because I know I can still do all things through Christ Who strengthens me. My life isn't dependent upon the things that are materially visible in this world, because they are not my source. God is my Source and He is my strength."

Paul gave warning about greed and covetousness in 1 Timothy, chapter 6:

> **Now godliness with contentment is great gain.**
>
> **For we brought nothing into this world, and it is certain we can carry nothing out.**
>
> **And having food and clothing, with these we shall be content.**
>
> **But those who desire to be rich fall into temptation and a snare, and into many foolish and harmful lusts which drown men in destruction and perdition.**
>
> **Verses 6-9**

Paul was saying, "This drive to be rich and to accumulate wealth will open the door to many foolish and hurtful lusts and unholy desires. The ultimate end is that people will turn their hearts away from God."

> *For the love of money is a root of all kinds of evil,* **for which some have strayed from the faith in their greediness, and pierced themselves through with many sorrows.**
>
> **But you, O man of God, flee these things and pursue righteousness, godliness, faith, love, patience, gentleness.**

Fight the good fight of faith, lay hold on eternal life, to which you were also called and have confessed the good confession in the presence of many witnesses.

Verses 10-12

God gave a warning in Deuteronomy 8:18,19 about remembering our Source, the One Who gives us the power to get wealth:

And you shall remember the Lord your God, for it is He who gives you power to get wealth, that He may establish His covenant which He swore to your fathers, as it is this day.

Then it shall be, if you by any means forget the Lord your God, and follow other gods, and serve them and worship them, I testify against you this day that you shall surely perish.

God makes His will for prosperity very clear in 3 John 2: **"Beloved, I pray that you may prosper in all things and be in health, just as your soul prospers."**

It is God's will that we live an abundant life, but it's a different thing when material gain and money create such a drive in people that it turns to covetousness.

The writer of Hebrews says:

Let your conduct be without covetousness; be content with such things as you have. For He Himself has said, "I will never leave you nor forsake you."

So we may boldly say: "The Lord is my helper; I will not fear. What can man do to me?"

Hebrews 13:5,6

53

A covetous person never reaches the point where he believes he has enough. He is always striving for more.

Lucifer Was Dominated by Covetousness

Lucifer, the covering archangel of God, was the most beautiful creature God had made up to that time. As the cherub of God, he led the worship in heaven. He had position, riches, and honor beyond any other angelic being, yet Ezekiel 28 and Isaiah 14 tell us that he came to a point where he was not content with his position. He wanted the glory and position of God Himself.

> **How art thou fallen from heaven, O Lucifer, son of the morning! how art thou cut down to the ground, which didst weaken the nations!**
>
> **For thou hast said in thine heart, I will ascend into heaven, I will exalt my throne above the stars of God: I will sit also upon the mount of the congregation, in the sides of the north:**
>
> **I will ascend above the heights of the clouds: I will be like the most High.**
>
> **Yet thou shalt be brought down to hell, to the sides of the pit.**
>
> **Isaiah 14:12-15 KJV**

Lucifer was thrown out of God's Kingdom forever because of covetousness.

Covetousness Caused Adam and Eve's Fall

Adam and Eve had dominion over the entire earth and the provision of everything they could ever desire. But God made one stipulation they were required to follow:

"Of every tree of the garden you may freely eat;

"But of the tree of the knowledge of good and evil you shall not eat, for in the day that you eat of it you shall surely die."

Genesis 2:16,17

A spirit of discontent came into Adam and Eve. Eve saw that the tree was good for food, it was beautiful and pleasant to the eyes, and it would make one wise. Yet, God had already made provision for everything they would ever need.

Adam and Eve took what did not belong to them and opened the door to the spirit of covetousness upon the whole world.

Solomon Was Enslaved by Covetousness

Covetousness got into the heart of another Old Testament leader — Solomon — who was honored as a man of great wisdom.

Solomon had 700 wives and 300 concubines. He allowed idol worship in Israel. Although God had said the Israelites were not to take heathen women in marriage, Solomon married the daughter of Pharaoh, who was a devil worshipper. At one point, idols and heathen worship were ordained by Solomon.

55

At the end of his life, Solomon had disobeyed God in marrying the wrong kind of women; amassing gold against God's strict orders, piling it up and gathering it from everywhere, spending more time building his own house than he spent building the temple of God, and opening trade to Egypt, an enemy.

Ecclesiastes, chapter 2, tells the story of the end of his life. This is a picture of what covetousness will do.

> **Whatever my eyes desired I did not keep from them. I did not withhold my heart from any pleasure, for my heart rejoiced in all my labor; and this was my reward from all my labor.**
>
> **Then I looked on all the works that my hands had done and on the labor in which I had toiled; and indeed all was vanity and grasping for the wind. There was no profit under the sun.**
>
> **Ecclesiastes 2:10,11**

Everything was vanity and empty.

Rich Young Ruler Bound by Covetousness

In the New Testament, the rich young ruler walked away from Jesus because he coveted the money that he possessed. Let's look at this account:

> **Now behold, one came and said to Him, "Good Teacher, what good thing shall I do that I may have eternal life?"**
>
> **So He said to him, "Why do you call Me good? No one is good but One, that is, God. But if you want to enter into life, keep the commandments."**

He said to Him, "Which ones?" Jesus said, " 'You shall not murder,' 'You shall not commit adultery,' 'You shall not steal,' 'You shall not bear false witness,'

" 'Honor your father and your mother,' and, 'You shall love your neighbor as yourself.' "

The young man said to Him, "All these things I have kept from my youth. What do I still lack?"

Jesus said to him, "If you want to be perfect, go, sell what you have and give to the poor, and you will have treasure in heaven; and come, follow Me."

But when the young man heard that saying, he went away sorrowful, for he had great possessions.

Matthew 19:16-22

The truth is, the possessions really had him!

Covetousness Has a Hold on Many Believers Today

Sometimes Christians cheat on income taxes because of a spirit of covetousness. Or they do not tithe and give offerings to God because they don't have faith that God will bless them if they give to Him. They hold on to what they have.

One of the things that will take many Christians out of this last-day revival is the spirit of covetousness. In the midst of revival, they will be entangled with the affairs of this life.

Sharon and I know of people who started out for God, but ended up out of the race of life because of covetousness. I think of one young man who had every-thing going for him as a Christian. But the desire for money drove him to do things and to live such a lifestyle that today, his marriage and his relationship with God are gone.

There is more to life than accumulating wealth. It is God's will that you prosper and be blessed, but you don't have to get into covetousness to have your needs met. You can get into God's plan of prosperity, which is seeking first the Kingdom of God and His righteousness, and God will bless you in *every area* of your life.

A man I had grown up with took a traveling sales job. After a few months, he recognized it was wrecking his relationship with God, with his wife, and with his chil-dren. He laid the job down and came home to take a lower-paying job. He learned to be content with what he had and to believe God to meet his needs. Even though he lost a job, he gained his family.

Perhaps a company has offered you a better job in a certain city if you will transfer. Historically, many people have transferred and taken those super offers, having never asked the Holy Ghost. They ended up getting burned, with a deterioration and sometimes complete brokenness and failure in their relationships with family and God.

Many mothers have left their children in their early stages of development to go to work, not because they needed the money in the home, but because of a spirit of covetousness.

So what do we need to do? We must do what the Word says. We can do *all things* through Christ. Whether we have an abundance or a lack makes no difference. We must do what God tells us to do and go where God tells us to go, because as we are obedient, *heaven's resources will come to us.*

The reason many young married couples split up is because of a spirit of covetousness that drives them to get into debt over their heads.

If you are at an income level where you can only afford a $150 or $200 apartment, then get in it and be content until God blesses you in another place. It is not prosperity for you to be in debt over your head and in bondage to the loan company. That is false prosperity. It is a deception. It has drowned men in their foolish lusts and even taken people away from God into perdition.

Years ago a young couple in our Body were very poor, but God started blessing them. The spirit of covetousness came in and they began to live for "things." The day came when they quit going to church to stay home and watch videos, because they had never had a video player.

The marriage and their finances fell apart, and only the grace of God brought them back together. Sharon and I had an opportunity to pray with them. It all goes back to a spirit of covetousness.

There is a revival going on, but if you are caught in the

throes of covetousness, you will never be where God wants you to be. You will miss it.

A young woman in our congregation came to us and said, "I am a single woman. I have lived with a consuming, driving thing in me to get married." (There is nothing wrong with desiring a husband, but when the spirit of covetousness comes in you, it blocks everything else.) She said, "It has consumed my life." She was set free from that driving spirit.

There is nothing wrong with having nice things, but when covetousness becomes a driving passion, causing you to sacrifice your morals to make more money, it is wrong.

Perhaps you have been tempted to work in restaurants and clubs selling alcohol and liquor because you can make big bucks on your tips. You may be a Christian when you carry alcohol to people, but you are a party to their becoming alcoholics.

If you are working in a convenience store and you are passing *Playboys* across the counter, how can you call yourself a Christian?

The prodigal son left home because he was not content in father's house. God's love never gives up on you, but friend, if the spirit of covetousness gets inside of you, you will walk away from God. God's love never stops, but the prodigal son walked away because he wanted "things."

This is an hour when the spirit of covetousness literally dominates America. It is a spirit that must be resisted, or else you can say you are a Christian, but in practice, you serve the god of this world.

God has a purpose for the drive, the energy, and the ambition in your life. His purpose is bigger than just making big bucks. God wants to use your talents, gifts, and abilities to build His Kingdom.

When the big bucks start to roll, many people get caught in the snowball. There is a reason for prosperity, but it's not to build bigger things for yourself. God's prosperity is to advance His Kingdom.

It's time for us to **"...lay aside every weight, and the sin which doth so easily beset us, and let us run with patience the race that is set before us, looking unto Jesus the author and finisher of our faith..."** (Hebrews 12:1,2 KJV).

We have addressed weights and sins that must be laid aside if you intend to run the race God has for you and win the prize. These weights and sins take your eyes off of Jesus. If you lose sight of Him, examine yourself and get back on track.

Wake up! *Heaven is on its feet!* Get free of every hindrance and run the race that God has set before you.

6

SPIRIT LED

In the summer of 1991, while at Lester Sumrall's Campmeeting, Dr. Sumrall shared about his upcoming August trip to Russia. My spirit lept with excitement at the thought that Sharon and I should go. When Dr. Sumrall said, "Why don't you go with me?" out of my spirit came, "Yes, Sir."

Then I tried to figure out how I was going to go because I was scheduled to do a TV taping in Israel on Wednesday of the same week. We flew to Israel on Monday, got there on Tuesday, filmed on Wednesday and left for St. Petersburg, Russia, on Thursday. I was to preach Saturday night in Dr. Sumrall's meeting.

As I sat in the service, the Spirit of God spoke inside of my heart that we were to return to St. Petersburg on a regular basis. Approximately 6,000 to 7,000 people were in attendance at Dr. Sumrall's meetings, but in the Spirit, I saw the huge indoor Sports Arena filled. I had such an urgency in me to return quickly.

Paul said to Timothy, **"Do your utmost to *come before winter...*"** (2 Timothy 4:21). There is a winter, an ending, a closing when the opportunity to share the gospel in every part of the world will be over. We must **"work the works of Him who sent** [us] **while it is day; the night is coming when no one can work"** (John 9:4).

The first opportunity to have a week-long crusade in Russia was November 1991. While I was in prayer on our flight back to Tulsa, the Lord took me to scripture that was unfamiliar to me.

> **For thus saith the Lord God, My people went down aforetime into Egypt to sojourn there; and the Assyrian oppressed them** *without cause*.
>
> **Isaiah 52:4** KJV

Parts of Russia were evangelized around the Eighth Century, which was delayed in comparison to the rest of Europe and the Mediterranean region. Paul had preached in the southern portion of Europe around the Mediterranean in the First Century.

Israel's trip into Egypt didn't begin in bondage. It began as they were looking for a better day. They went into Egypt to get grain. Joseph invited his family there, and Pharaoh gave them the land of Goshen.

The Lord spoke to me, "Russia went into Egypt (Communism) basically for grain. Initially, they weren't in bondage."

Around 1917, the Soviet Union's leaders began to propagate the idea of the people working together for common good based upon Marx's theories. They reasoned that if they had the rule of the state and everyone was on the same level, they wouldn't have the hierarchy of the rich and the poor. Russia went into Communism.

In 1922 when Stalin came to power, instead of Communism being a liberating philosophy, it became a severe oppression. Under his rule, millions of people were either killed or sent to Siberian labor camps. Though the Russian people did no wrong, they were under terrible oppression.

> **Now therefore, what have I here, saith the Lord, that my people is taken away for nought? they that rule over them make them to howl, saith the Lord; and my name continually every day is blasphemed.**
>
> **Isaiah 52:5 KJV**

Included in the entire educational process in Russia for over seventy years was the teaching, "There is no God."

I continued to read from Isaiah 52:

> **Therefore my people shall know my name: therefore they shall know in that day that I am he that doth speak: behold, it is I.**
>
> **How beautiful upon the mountains are the feet of him that bringeth good tidings, that publisheth peace; that bringeth good tidings of good, that publisheth salvation; that saith unto Zion, Thy God reigneth!**
>
> **Verses 6,7 KJV**

God spoke to my heart, "I am calling you to go into Russia at this time." I announced to our congregation the following Sunday, "We are going back to Russia in November."

We sent faxes to the one church organization we knew in St. Petersburg to help us make arrangements for a November crusade. It took about two weeks to get a response: "We don't think you should come for a year, because we have so many situations we are trying to resolve." Yet, I had the word of the Lord, "Go quickly" and "Come before winter."

We made contact with other people in St. Petersburg, and they said the same thing: "Wait." After receiving absolutely no encouragement to return to Russia from our contacts in St. Petersburg, I gave my file of information on Russia to my secretary and said, "File it away. They don't feel we should come right now." That was in September 1991.

During that same week, inside of my spirit kept coming, "The door is open now. You have a narrow space of time. It is urgent that you go through it quickly." It kept getting stronger in my spirit. I'm talking to you about being led by the Spirit of God.

On Sunday morning in late September 1991, when I was getting ready for church, I couldn't get my mind on what I was going to preach. I kept thinking about going back to Russia. Finally, I said to Sharon, "We are going to go in November anyway. We don't know anyone. We don't have anyone to work with, but God will work it out."

After I preached and ministered to the people, I was shaking hands with members of my congregation when four people walked up to me and said in broken English, "We hear you are going to St. Petersburg, Russia. We would like to help you." I had never seen them before or had any contact with them. Three of them were ministers. They were all from St. Petersburg and had contact with four churches in Russia, in addition to the one church we knew.

It is so important to be led by the Holy Spirit. At our first meeting in St. Petersburg in November 1991, 25,584 people gave their hearts to Jesus Christ. *At the end of our obedience was salvation for many.*

Some people look at being led by the Holy Spirit as a type of game that is nice, and you are happy, blessed, peaceful, and benefited, but you need to see it from God's perspective. If you have the truth and the light and God is leading you, He will lead you to people who are in darkness and are bound by ignorance, unbelief, tradition, denominationalism, or blindness. He will lead you to take His truth, light, help, hope, and strength that you have to set others free.

Go with what is in your spirit. Go with what is deep in your heart. You may be asking, "How do I know what is deep in my heart?" By practicing the presence of Jesus, acknowledging Him, seeking Him and drawing near to Him. If you desire the leading of the Holy Spirit, He will guide you in all the affairs of life.

To be led by His Spirit requires a commitment of your *time* in the Word, in prayer, and in quiet before Him.

You will know God's leading by the inward witness. You will know it by peace. You will know it by the Holy Spirit. You will know it by the Word of God. If something is your own idea or the input of another person, it will fade, but something from the Holy Spirit will keep getting stronger and more intense inside of you.

At the end of being led by the Holy Spirit — just as with our experience in St. Petersburg — there are souls to be saved. We are in the day of God's great harvest in all the earth.

7

TAKING ON A "POSSESS THE LAND" MENTALITY

When I speak of the "Church of the Lord Jesus Christ," I am referring to the *people* who make up the Church.

A militant church is a people who know how to fight an effective warfare, taking dominion over every work of the devil as opposed to a position of passivity the Church has held for so long. The militant church moves from the stance of indifference to motivation, from inactivity to activity, and from passivity to aggressiveness.

When we use the word *military* or *militant*, or the term, *possess the land mentality*, we are speaking of people who are trained and prepared to either defend their country or to advance in war or in battle. The Church, as a whole, has not been in a posture of militancy, but rather in a posture of indifference, as if there were no conflict, carrying on business as usual.

The problem with this is that we have an enemy who knows nothing about peace time. No truce has been signed. It's clear from Scripture that Jesus destroyed the power and authority of the devil, but He did not destroy the devil.

Jesus did not annihilate the devil or obliterate him from existence. He took the keys back from him, but it's very clear in the New Testament that the devil still goes about **"...like a roaring lion, seeking whom he may devour"** (1 Peter 5:8).

Even though Jesus took the keys of hell and death from the devil and He has given every believer full authority over him, the devil is still a very real foe. When God said to the children of Israel, "I am giving you a land flowing with milk and honey," had God already driven out all the enemies that were in that land? No. He gave the Israelites the land, but they had to go in and possess it. They had to drive out the enemies, which is a pattern for believers to follow today. God has given us an inheritance, and He has given us a land, but we must possess it. He will destroy the enemies, but only as we march forward, taking dominion in Jesus' name.

The children of Israel were terrified when they came to the promised land and they saw the giants and the walled cities. They felt overwhelmed. Two of the spies came back with a good report, while ten of the twelve brought back an evil report. The Israelites believed the evil report of the majority. As a result, they did not enter the promised land, but they limited the Holy One of Israel. You can limit God by doubt and unbelief. Because the Israelites turned back from the promised land, they spent forty years wandering in the wilderness.

It did not take the Israelites forty years to get from Egypt to the edge of the promised land. It only took a matter of months, and a large part of that time was constructing the tabernacle, receiving the ordinances and laws of God and setting themselves in order. When they came to the edge of the land of Canaan, they rebelled, turned back, doubted God and spent forty years in the wilderness.

As a result of turning their backs on God, everyone twenty years of age and upward died in the wilderness. Those under twenty years of age became Joshua's warriors, the fighting men of that day.

Let's examine this account in Joshua 1:1-9:

> **After the death of Moses the servant of the Lord, it came to pass that the Lord spoke to Joshua the son of Nun, Moses' assistant, saying:**
>
> **"Moses My servant is dead. Now therefore, arise, go over this Jordan, you and all this people, to the land which I am giving to them — the children of Israel.**
>
> **"Every place that the sole of your foot will tread upon I have given you, as I said to Moses.**
>
> **"From the wilderness and this Lebanon as far as the great river, the River Euphrates, all the land of the Hittites, and to the Great Sea toward the going down of the sun, shall be your territory.**
>
> **"No man shall be able to stand before you all the days of your life; as I was with Moses, so I will be with you. I will not leave you nor forsake you.**
>
> **"Be strong and of good courage, for to this people you shall divide as an inheritance the land which I swore to their fathers to give them.**

"Only be strong and very courageous, that you may observe to do according to all the law which Moses My servant commanded you; do not turn from it to the right hand or to the left, that you may prosper wherever you go.

"This Book of the Law shall not depart from your mouth, but you shall meditate in it day and night, that you may observe to do according to all that is written in it. For then you will make your way prosperous, and then you will have good success.

"Have I not commanded you? Be strong and of good courage; do not be afraid, nor be dismayed, for the Lord your God is with you wherever you go."

This was a word given to Joshua and his warriors that they would be an invading force. The Church today is to be an *invading force*, going into what Satan thinks is his turf and retrieving those who will be saved.

We have been given land that we are to possess. Psalm 24:1 says, **"The earth is the Lord's, and all its fullness, the world and those who dwell therein."**

God gave Adam and the generations that would follow him a commission to **"Be fruitful and multiply; fill the earth and subdue it; have dominion over the fish of the sea, over the birds of the air, and over every living thing that moves on the earth"** (Genesis 1:28). That was the first commission. No part of the earth belongs to the devil. All of our cities belong to God.

There are places God has called the Church at large to go and make a difference. One of the things the Lord spoke to Victory Christian Center specifically as a Body was, "Go to the government-subsidized apartment communities in your area that are infested with poverty, crime, evil, immorality, drug addiction, and child abuse. Invade those places and declare in the realm of the spirit, 'Jesus is Lord.' Then go door-to-door and bring those people to Me."

Hundreds of people have been born again because of that effort, but we have only begun. The Church must be moved out of a country club or a social club mentality.

You don't go to church just to salve your conscience and associate. You go to church to be trained and armed for doing the works of Jesus. It's time to rise out of complacency that causes a person to say, "Who cares? Big deal! I've got my own problems. Why do I need to stir up any more things?" That's the attitude of many people. They don't want to get involved.

Not everyone is called into the same arena of ministry, but everyone is called to serve. Everyone is to be a part of the effort. Some are called into the battle of intercession.

Because of fear, some people are holding back from taking the necessary steps to invade the areas of darkness around them. One of the areas we must attack is perversion, which is a demonic spirit. Jesus Christ of Nazareth can deliver homosexuals. When we speak God's Word and command that spirit to leave the people who desire to be free of it, it has no choice but to go.

Alcoholism, drug addiction, and abortion are realms

of the enemy that must be invaded in this hour. This is not a time of complacency or fear. It is a time to move!

The mentality of many people must be changed. Some people are paralyzed in their traditional posture because there has been a mentality of just holding the fort and staying where we are.

When you look at the Church at large, few people have seen it as an invading force that will defeat the powers of darkness.

Our Battle Is Not with Flesh and Blood

When I speak about an attitude of militancy, I'm not talking about registering to carry a gun or loading your shotgun to straighten out some of the drug peddlers. I am talking about a battle in the realm of the spirit. Our battle is not with flesh and blood, but with principalities and powers.

> **Finally, my brethren, be strong in the Lord and in the power of His might.**
>
> **Ephesians 6:10**

There are demonstrations of power that can be seen in military parades, but Paul isn't talking about a natural demonstration of strength. Our strength must be in the Lord. We are not battling against human beings. We are battling against wicked principalities and powers. Our war is in the spirit realm.

> **Put on the whole armor of God, that you may be able to stand against the wiles of the devil.**
>
> **Ephesians 6:11**

Paul is saying to put on our spiritual armor daily, because we are in a continual conflict with the devil.

There are many similarities between Ephesians 6 and Joshua 1. Joshua and Paul both spoke of God's warriors.

The devil has a terrible plan for your life. The summation of his plan is to steal, kill and destroy you (John 10:10).

Paul is saying, "If you are to stand against the devil's plan to steal from you, to kill you, and to destroy your home, your family, your nation, and your city, you have to put on the whole armor of God. You must get in the right attitude."

Paul isn't talking about some little game. He is saying, "The devil has a horrible plan for your life. If you are going to withstand his plans, plots, and schemes to steal, kill, and destroy, everything that you have and everything you know that is good, then you must be prepared, both defensively and offensively.

> **For we do not wrestle against flesh and blood, but against principalities, against powers, against the rulers of the darkness of this age, against spiritual hosts of wickedness in the heavenly places.**
>
> **Ephesians 6:12**

Paul defines a satanic military order of generals, lieutenants, colonels, and sergeants who are in the unseen realm of the atmosphere around us. Lucifer, the rebellious angel who left the presence of God, was cast out of heaven, and he has demon spirits, wicked principalities and powers under his command. His demonic forces are arrayed to manipulate, influence, and control circumstances and people in the earth, like puppets on a string.

As God's children, we are to be controlled and moved by *the Spirit of God*. We are to move in direct opposition to the forces of the devil.

Paul talks about putting on the whole spiritual armor: girding the loins with truth; putting on the breastplate of righteousness; the preparation of the gospel of peace upon your feet; the helmet of salvation; the shield of faith, and the sword of the Spirit, which is the Word of God; praying always with all prayer and supplication in the Holy Spirit. Paul says this armor is necessary to win in the Christian life.

Let's look at verses 13-18:

Therefore take up the whole armor of God, that you may be able to withstand in the evil day, and having done all, to stand.

Stand therefore, having girded your waist with truth, having put on the breastplate of righteousness,

And having shod your feet with the preparation of the gospel of peace;

Above all, taking the shield of faith with which you will be able to quench all the fiery darts of the wicked one.

> And take the helmet of salvation, and the sword of the Spirit, which is the word of God;
>
> Praying always with all prayer and supplication in the Spirit, being watchful to this end with all perseverance and supplication for all the saints.

Pulling Down Strongholds

Second Corinthians 10:4 says, **"For the weapons of our warfare are not carnal but mighty in God for pulling down strongholds."**

Some of the strongholds that need to be pulled down in our society are pornography, divorce, child abuse, prostitution, AIDS, drug abuse, prejudice, suicide, the occult, poverty, religion, the New Age Movement, witchcraft, and mental problems.

There are spiritual prisoners of war in each of these areas who must be liberated. I pray you will hear the cry of these prisoners. If we are going to change our society, we must change the hearts of people.

Proclaiming God's Kingdom

God's Kingdom is what we must proclaim to deliver people. We are called to bring deliverance to people. You may say, "I'm not a minister." The Bible says every believer is a minister of God. *Minister* means "servant," and we'll talk more about the heart of a servant in a later chapter.

Acts 1:8 says, **"But you shall receive power when the Holy Spirit has come upon you; and you shall be witnesses to Me in Jerusalem, and in all Judea and Samaria, and to the end of the earth."**

To witness of Jesus is to "tell." To preach is to "proclaim." You are called to tell and proclaim. You may not be preaching from a pulpit, but every person has a platform. It's time that you recognize your calling and your responsibility and do what you are called to do.

The Church must go after the prisoners of war. The Church must go after the powers and principalities of darkness that have controlled people's lives. It's no time to sit back and wait. There's a mentality that says, "If the Lord wants me to do it, then it will happen." Some people have been waiting for fifty years for God to do it. He has told us to be witnesses. When the Lord gives you the direction of what to do, go into action and make it happen!

When you study the book of Joshua, you will find that the Israelites had to cross the Jordan. As they took the steps to cross the Jordan, only then did the Jordan divide. That river did *not* divide until the priests marched into the water and got their feet wet. In other words, *miracles rarely happen until you move into action.*

We didn't get the money to build our own ministry facilities until we found out what God wanted us to do. Then we started praying and believing. We started with what we had at that time. God told us to give away what we had, and as we obeyed, God made a way.

What are you waiting on? Maybe God has called you into full-time ministry and you are waiting on the Lord. I say, "Why sit ye here until you die?"

There are plenty of places to preach. There are opportunities to preach in nursing homes, jails, ghettos, and the streets. If we can win the battle with the little children, we can save teenagers from drug addiction. We can save many marriages if we teach children how to walk in love and forgiveness. Pride is the main reason for divorce, and if we can deal with submission, humility, and discernment when people are young, and how to listen to the Holy Spirit in selecting a mate, we can drastically lower the divorce statistics.

God called us to have a "possess the land" mentality — to move out of our comfort zone into conflict with enemy forces.

We are *not* called to sit back in lethargy and complacency. We are called to march forward. We are not called to relax on our laurels or on our achievements, but we are called to hear the cry of the prisoners and loose them. A good place to begin is with prayer, which we will discuss in the next chapter.

8

ANSWERING THE CALL TO PRAYER

Every believer is called to prayer — corporately and individually. Your prayer life reveals how much you depend on God and also how much you depend upon yourself. Your prayer life is an indicator of where you place your trust.

John Wesley said that it seems that God does nothing but that someone prays. It was his belief, and Scripture confirms it, that God moves in response to prayer.

Dr. Lester Sumrall told the story of becoming deathly ill as a young missionary and falling from his mule as he rode over the mountains of Tibet. Since he was the last person in the mule train, no one noticed that he had fallen and was left behind.

After a few hours of being unconsciousness, he awakened totally refreshed and healed. He got back on the mule, and amazingly, the mule led him on to the little village where the rest of the team spent the night.

A year later when he was back in the states, he met a little prayer warrior who opened up her diary and asked him what he was doing on a particular day at such and such a time. She had written in her diary when God spoke to her, "Lester Sumrall is dying. Pray." She had been awakened by the Spirit of God and had prayed, and God delivered Lester Sumrall. Thank God for prayer! It can make the difference between life and death.

Andrew Murray said that the neglect of quiet communion with Jesus every morning is generally the primary cause of failure.`

Martin Luther said if he neglected prayer but a single day, he would lose a great deal of the fire of faith.

If there is anything that we should be doing as Christians in this hour, *we should be praying*. The truth about prayer is found in the Word of God.

For the word of God is living and powerful, and sharper than any two-edged sword, piercing even to the division of soul and spirit, and of joints and marrow, and is a discerner of the thoughts and intents of the heart.

And there is no creature hidden from His sight, but all things are naked and open to the eyes of Him to whom we must give account.

Seeing then that we have a great High Priest who has passed through the heavens, Jesus the Son of God, let us hold fast our confession.

For we do not have a High Priest who cannot sympathize with our weaknesses, but was in all points tempted as we are, yet without sin.

Let us therefore come boldly to the throne of grace,

that we may obtain mercy and find grace to help in time of need.

Hebrews 4:12-16

When our house caught on fire the night of October 22, 1991, we later learned that many people were awakened by the Spirit of God between 1:30 and 2:00 in the morning and began to pray for us. A spirit of intercession hit one family the previous evening as they were having their family devotions, so they prayed for us.

We talked with one of the firemen who is involved with the investigation of fires. His words to us were, "You are so lucky! We go to fires that are of much less magnitude where the people die from smoke inhalation." Then he said, "When I walked into your house, I could not imagine anyone getting out alive."

The fire chief in charge said the smoke damage was about as severe as any he had seen in the city of Tulsa. The smoke blanketed the house, under the beds, even in the areas that were not totally burned. The chief said they sent an extra truck with workers just to go in and recover the bodies. He said, "We could not believe that you were all out."

As we walked back through the house and saw where the fire burned, we realized we were probably thirty seconds away from death, but God brought us out. I believe our own prayers made a difference, but I also believe the prayers of other people made a difference.

Perhaps you, too, have had narrow escapes, some that you are aware of to a degree and others that you may not be aware of, where the Spirit of God caused someone to pray, and God sent His angels for deliverance and protection.

You Can Dial Direct!

Because of what Jesus has done, *you have direct access into the throne room of God.* Jesus died on the cross, shed His blood and was buried, and on the third day He was raised from the dead. He then took His own blood and placed it on the mercy seat. We have a type of that in the Old Testament tabernacle under Moses and later in the temple under Solomon, where the high priest took the blood of an animal sacrifice, and through the blood, entered into the Holy of Holies.

Jesus is our High Priest. He entered in once and for all for all people. Now He has opened the door to heaven for all of us to come into the very throne room of God. We aren't just trying to get in contact with God through long distance. We aren't trying to get an appointment with Him or gain entry to Him. Jesus has already made the entry for us. He has already opened the door.

Scripture says Jesus was tempted in all points just like we are, so we aren't talking to Someone Who can't relate or Who is disinterested. We are talking about Someone Who has been where we are, Who cares and understands. His name is Jesus Christ of Nazareth.

The writer of Hebrews said, **"Let us therefore come boldly to the throne of grace, that we may obtain mercy and find grace to help in time of need"** (Hebrews 4:16).

To come *boldly* means to come with confidence, assurance, and courage. You can come boldly because you have faith that the blood of Jesus cleanses you from all sin and that you are forgiven. You can come with confidence, not cowering in fear, intimidation, or condemnation. You can come directly into the throne room to obtain God's mercy and help in the time of your need.

Prayer can be the prayer of worship or it can be the prayer of praise and communion — just talking with God and listening to Him. In Hebrews 4, the writer specifically talks about the prayer to get God's help, His grace, His mercy, and His benefits into our lives.

Pray in Faith According to the Word

Prayer that is not according to the Word of God will not produce results. If we are going to receive God's answers, we must be in tune with His thoughts so that our thinking is in line with His thinking and our hearts are in line with His heart.

> **For the word of God is living and powerful, and sharper than any two-edged sword....**
>
> **Hebrews 4:12**

The Word of God will reveal your thoughts. It will divide between what is of the soul and that which is truly of the Spirit. How do you know if you are praying out of your own desires or out of the heart and desires of God? The Word will distinguish between your own desires and God's desires.

Psalm 37:4 says, **"Delight yourself also in the Lord, and He shall give you the desires of your heart."**

Many times we think this is just the granting of our desires, but there is another side to it: the implanting of His desires so that we have the right desires. We get right desires by *delighting ourselves in God's Word.*

In John 15:7 Jesus said, **"If you abide in Me, and My words abide in you, you will *ask what you desire*, and it shall be done for you."**

Why does prayer go unanswered for many people? They aren't abiding in communion with God. There is no Word inside of them, so they pray hit-and-miss prayers. They are like a boy with a ball, tossing one up, seeing if God will catch it.

People say, "I have prayed and nothing has happened." God says, "If you will abide in Me and My words abide in you, you will ask what you will and *it shall be done.*" That is a 100 percent positive promise. God is not a man that He should lie (Numbers 23:19).

Second Chronicles 7:14 says:

"If My people who are called by My name will humble themselves, and pray and seek My face, and turn from

their wicked ways, then I will hear from heaven, and will
forgive their sin and heal their land."

It is the will of God in this hour that we seek His face,
that we pray His will in heaven into the earth, beginning
with our own lives, including the family, the church, the
states, the nation, and ultimately, the world.

You may think satellite is fast, but with prayer, we can
touch any nation of the world the moment we pray. God
hears and dispatches His angels.

God dispatched His angels on Daniel's behalf *the
moment Daniel prayed*. For twenty-one days, there was
seemingly no answer, but when the angel appeared to
Daniel, he said:

> **"O Daniel, man greatly beloved, understand the
> words that I speak to you, and stand upright, for I have
> now been sent to you." While he was speaking this word
> to me, I stood trembling.**
>
> **Then he said to me, "Do not fear, Daniel, for from
> the first day that you set your heart to understand, and
> to humble yourself before your God, *your words were
> heard; and I have come because of your words*.**
>
> **"But the prince of the kingdom of Persia withstood
> me twenty-one days; and behold, Michael, one of the chief
> princes, came to help me, for I had been left alone there
> with the kings of Persia."**
>
> **Daniel 10:11-13**

Just as the angels came because of Daniel's words, God

responds to our words. This is why our words must be aligned with God's Word.

Sometimes people talk about prayer being silent and meditative. I believe there is a communion with God where we get into the Spirit and we hear God's voice, but remember, the angels come *because of our words*. They come when we pray and speak the Word which is alive, powerful, and sharper than any two-edged sword.

God's Word rises up inside of us because it is alive and because we bring it back to Him in prayer.

Hold Fast the Confession of Your Faith

God says in Jeremiah 1:12 KJV, **"...I will hasten my word to perform it."** He watches over His Word to bring it to pass. The Word is like seed that is sown. As we believe it and speak it, it will bring forth, first the blade, then the ear, then the full corn in the ear.

Hebrews 10:23 KJV says, **"Let us hold fast the profession of our faith without wavering; (for he is faithful that promised)."**

Once you have prayed, it is important that you continue to hold fast to that which you have spoken in line with God's Word.

A couple in our church were given a diagnosis that the baby in the wife's womb was dead. The wife came to Sharon and asked what she should do, because doctors wanted to abort the baby. Sharon prayed with her, then encouraged her to go back for a second examination. As she was examined again, it was discovered that the baby was alive.

To speak God's Word in prayer is powerful. The battle in prayer is whether we are going to agree and speak the words of the world, the words of the circumstances, *or* the Word of God.

Mix Faith with the Word

When you take God's Word to Him in prayer, it must be mixed with faith to produce results. Hebrews 4:2 says of the children of Israel: **"...the word which they heard did not profit them, not being mixed with faith in those who heard it."**

Prayer without faith is like a boat without oars or a car without gasoline. It won't go anywhere. It is the faith inside of you that makes prayer effective.

How does faith come? Romans 10:17 says, **"...faith comes by hearing, and hearing by the word of God."**

It is faith in God that brings God on the scene.

First John 5:14,15 says:

Now this is the confidence that we have in Him, that if we ask anything *according to His will*, He hears us.

And if we know that He hears us, whatever we ask, we know that we have the petitions that we have asked of Him.

What is God's will? God's Word is His will. When you

are praying for specific things, first find the promises in God's Word that grant the particular request you are making.

In one of our services, a young man testified of praying for the salvation of an unsaved family member who was then saved. I asked him to lead in prayer for the salvation of loved ones. A woman in the service, who later shared with us, stood for the salvation of her sister.

When we prayed and believed that we received, the young man said, "Try to make contact this week with the people you prayed for." That night, this woman called her sister who said, "I was born again at church tonight."

What do you do if your prayers aren't answered immediately? Hold fast to your confession of God's Word. Hold fast to what you have prayed and spoken. Don't let go of it. *Don't change and say,* "I guess it's not working. Nothing is happening. The symptoms haven't changed. There are no more finances. There is no change in the situation in the company."

Whatever area it is, don't uproot your good seed with words of doubt and unbelief. *Continue to water your prayers with the continual confession of what God says in His Word.*

This is the confidence we have if we ask according to His will, He hears us, and if He hears us, our answers are assured.

Sharon and I were at Christ For The Nations several

years ago when Freda Lindsay asked that we corporately pray for one of the student body members who was about to give birth to a baby. Unless there was a miraculous, immediate turning in the womb, the baby would be born breach. Mrs. Lindsay said, "We need to pray for this baby to turn around. Doctors are going to make a decision in one hour as to what they will do."

Before that Sunday afternoon meeting was over, we received word that the baby had turned and was delivered healthy and normal. God can turn all things around when we pray!

Mark 11:24 KJV says, **"Therefore I say unto you, What things soever ye desire, when ye pray, believe that ye receive them, and ye shall have them."**

How can you believe that you receive something when you pray if you're not sure it is God's will? You simply can't. Some people have a struggle with faith, because they haven't understood the importance of praying according to God's Word, taking His promises and speaking them aloud, bringing them to the Father. The Word is alive and powerful. God watches over His Word. Delight, abide, and dwell in it, bringing it to Him in prayer. Then when you pray, believe that you receive, even before you see the manifestation of it.

Second Corinthians 5:7 says, **"For we walk by faith, not by sight."** Our eyes are not on temporal things. They are on eternal things. The most eternal thing you can look at today is the Word of God.

Pray About Everything

Philippians 4:6,7 says:

Be anxious for nothing, but in everything by prayer and supplication, with thanksgiving, let your requests be made known to God;

And the peace of God, which surpasses all understanding, will guard your hearts and minds through Christ Jesus.

Anything that is big or little enough to worry about is big or little enough to pray about.

A friend told the story about going to a large Methodist Conference years ago. A number of theologians were on a panel to speak in one session.

A charismatic Methodist pastor's wife, on fire for the Lord, lost the buckle on her shoe, and she was walking down the hall, praying and looking for it. One minister asked, "May I help you?" She said, "I am praying to find my shoe buckle."

He didn't say anything, but he looked around and then walked on. He was on the podium with the panel of speakers, and they were talking on the subject of prayer. He said, "I can't believe that someone would bother the God of the universe with a shoe buckle." He belittled the woman.

Oral Roberts was on the same panel, and when it was his turn to speak, he said, "God is concerned with anything that concerns you." He encouraged people to pray about everything, even lost shoe buckles.

God is big enough to take care of the little things. He has proven that. He turned the water into wine at the wedding in Cana. He multiplied the loaves and the fishes when the people could have gone home to eat. They wouldn't have starved. It was a matter of comfort in their lives, and yet Jesus met the need.

God is concerned about practical, personal things in your life. You can pray about everything. Don't let the devil talk you out of it.

Pray with Thanksgiving

Scripture says, **"...in every thing by prayer and supplication** *with thanksgiving* **let your requests be made known unto God"** (Philippians 4:6 KJV).

How can you thank God when you pray if you don't know the answer is on the way? You can't! But when you ask according to His will and believe that you receive, you can thank Him in advance.

Some people say, "Nothing has changed. I don't see any results. What do I do now?" Keep on thanking God. Every time the thought of worry comes to you, remember what Paul said: **"...the peace of God...will guard your hearts and minds through Christ Jesus"** (Philippians 4:7). **"Casting all your care upon Him, for He cares for you"** (1 Peter 5:7).

93

God is interested in you and concerned about you, so roll your cares and worries on Him. Then thank Him on a continual basis.

Pray to the Father in Jesus' Name

John 14:13,14 says:

> **And whatever you ask in My name, that I will do, that the Father may be glorified in the Son.**
>
> **If you ask anything in My name, I will do it.**

John 16:23,24 says basically the same thing:

> **And in that day you will ask Me nothing. Most assuredly, I say to you, whatever you ask the Father in My name He will give you.**
>
> **Until now you have asked nothing in My name. Ask, and you will receive, that your joy may be full.**

Prayer is to be made to the Father in the name of Jesus. Jesus' name is the key which unlocks all of heaven's benefits, and that name has been given to every believer.

Pray for Others

There is another key I want to share with you and that is to pray for others. Job 42:10 KJV says, **"And the Lord turned the captivity of Job, when he prayed for his friends: also the Lord gave Job twice as much as he had before."**

James 5:16 says, **"...Pray for one another, that you may be healed...."**

Just as there is a law of sowing and reaping in finances, there is a law of sowing and reaping in prayer. If you have needs in your own life, pray for someone else. As you give out, you will receive back into your own life. Let your prayers go beyond your life, beyond your family, and even beyond your church. As your prayers go outward, you are praying the same way Jesus prayed.

Psalm 2:8 says, **"Ask of Me, and I will give You the nations for Your inheritance, and the ends of the earth for Your possession."** The *King James Version* says, **"Ask of me, and I shall give thee the heathen for thine inheritance, and the uttermost parts of the earth for thy possession."**

Jesus Christ is daily interceding for the nations — for people throughout the world — and when we pray for nations, we move into that same flow. When we begin to move into that realm in prayer, our own needs will be met.

Matthew 6:31-33 applies to finances as well as to prayer. If you will seek God's Kingdom first in your prayers, then all the things you need will be added unto you.

When You Pray, Forgive

The verse that says we are to believe we receive when we pray is followed by two verses about forgiveness.

And whenever you stand praying, if you have anything against anyone, forgive him, that your Father in heaven may also forgive you your trespasses.

> **But if you do not forgive, neither will your Father in heaven forgive your trespasses.**
>
> **Mark 11:25,26**

If you are harboring unforgiveness, your prayers will not work. Galatians 5:6 says that faith works by love. Sometimes people say, "My prayers aren't working." Are you harboring bitterness or resentment?

A young woman who had been deathly ill and had the finest of medical help and treatment, showed no improvement in her condition. She was in continual torment. She cried out, "Lord, what is wrong?" The Lord spoke to her, "It is bitterness and resentment you have harbored toward a certain person."

As she repented, the presence of Jesus filled her hospital room, and in a matter of fifteen minutes (after months of sickness), all of the symptoms left and she rose up healed.

Prayer interconnects with the rest of your life: how you treat people and your attitudes toward people. Sometimes people try to separate it into a neat formula to do this and that, but it doesn't work. Prayer is involved with the whole of your Christianity.

Without the Word and Prayer, You Are Open Prey to the Enemy

If God does not inhabit your life, another spirit will. **"If you abide in Me, and My words abide in you, you will ask what you desire, and it shall be done for you"** (John 15:7).

Some people sit in church and play Christianity. They look and act the part, but you say, "Read the Bible," and they don't have a Bible. You say, "Pray" and they respond, "I just go to church. I am obligated to be there once a week."

You may be fooling yourself, but you are not fooling God or the devil. Without the Word and prayer, your life is open prey to the enemy. I say this out of a heart of love for you. If there is no Word and no prayer power in your life, you will have the enemy on your own turf.

Without the power of prayer in your life, you are no match for the devil. His schemes, plots, and trickery go beyond your ability in the natural to resist. But God is on your side. Greater is He Who is in you than he who is in the world (1 John 4:4). If God is for you, who can be against you? You can't lose if you will stay hooked up with Jesus Christ.

This is an hour for intensity in prayer. It's not an option to pray and read the Word. We are at the close of the Church age. Because the devil knows his time is short, he has come with great fury (Revelation 12:12). We are seeing it in the earth. I admonish you to be diligent in the Word and in prayer.

9

POSSESSING A SERVANT'S HEART

Paul personally trained Timothy as a warrior in the Lord. In today's vernacular, we would say that Paul was Timothy's mentor.

Paul said to Timothy:

> **Stir up the gift of God which is in you through the laying on of my hands.**
>
> **For God has not given us a spirit of fear, but of power and of love and of a sound mind.**
>
> **2 Timothy 1:6,7**

In another passage, Paul wrote of Timothy:

> **I hope in the Lord Jesus to send Timothy to you soon, that I also may be cheered when I receive news about you. I have no one else like him, who takes a genuine interest in your welfare. For everyone looks out for his own interests, not those of Jesus Christ. But you know that Timothy has proved himself, because *as a son with his father he has served with me in the work of the gospel.* I hope, therefore, to send him as soon as I see how things go with me.**
>
> **Philippians 2:19-23** NIV

In 64 A.D., Paul was in his first imprisonment in Rome. He was deeply concerned about the Christians at Philippi, because persecution was on the increase. I believe he wondered, *Will they remain true, or will they buckle under the persecution?* That's the real question with Christians today. Paul saw the handwriting on the wall. He knew what was coming, and he knew that he would give his life for the cause of Christ.

Paul wrote how, even in his chains, he had been able to testify and witness. He wrote to the Philippians, instructing them to *rejoice* regardless of the situations they faced. (*Rejoice* is the theme word in the book of Philippians.) Remember, Paul had been in chains on the first trip to Philippi, and he had seen God snap the chains when he and Silas praised Him at midnight.

Now, he basically said, "I would really like to be there with you. I would like to know what your condition is, both spiritually and naturally. I can't come, but I am sending Timothy to you for two reasons: 1) Timothy will cheer you up and he will encourage you; and 2) At the same time, when I receive news of how you are doing, it will cheer me up." Then Paul made a comment about Timothy that is very important for us to hear.

> **I have no one else like him** [Timothy], *who takes a genuine interest in your welfare.*
>
> **Philippians 2:20 NIV**

In Oklahoma, we would say, "He is the only one who

really cares about you. He has the same heart that I have for you, so I want to send him to you."

Then Paul made a comment about the rest of the Christians of that day. **"For everyone looks out for his own interests, not those of Jesus Christ"** (Philippians 2:21 NIV). Paul was writing about *selfish* Christians — people who were only concerned about themselves.

Paul was saying, "They are busy, but they are busy about their own things. I only have one person who is able to get free to come and minister to you, not because he doesn't have his own things to do, but because he has set a priority that you are more important than 'things.' He has just as many things to do, but Timothy is genuinely interested in your welfare. Timothy has proven his heart for the gospel and for you." The two are tied together. If you love the gospel, you will love the people for whom Jesus died. You cannot separate them.

Timothy had served with Paul in proclaiming this Good News. After you reach people, it doesn't end there, because people need to be trained, edified, built up, and strengthened. Timothy had evidence of these things working in his life as he served alongside Paul. Paul said, **"...as a son with his father he** [Timothy] **has served with me in the work of the gospel"** (Philippians 2:22 NIV).

I am praying that God will give many Timothys to the Body of Christ in this hour – *people who will care for people and who are willing to serve them.*

When you are born again, you take on a new nature. Your old nature of selfishness is gone, and your new nature is the nature of love. Whoever is born of God is born of love. Out of your new nature of the Spirit, you will care for the interests of other people. Your circle of interest will go beyond your own home, your business, your family, and your things. Your circle will be enlarged to include the entire Body of Christ.

My challenge to you is, "Enlarge your circle of love." Many people love, but it stops with their wife, their husband, their kids, their job, and their house. Paul was saying, "Timothy's love goes further. He is interested in other people."

Think about it. Timothy was willing to go where he was needed. He didn't have his own agenda. He was willing to submit, to work with and flow through the apostolic calling and anointing of Paul.

Jesus Is Calling Believers To Serve Others

Many people are waiting on their ministry or waiting for a wide door to open with a big name on it — a title, prestige, and position. It is as if Jesus is saying, "There's a towel and a wash basin. I have a place for you when you are ready to wash feet." That's the example He left to His disciples — serving and ministering to one another. As He washed their feet, He talked about serving in ministry.

When Jesus finished washing the disciples' feet, He said:

> **"Do you understand what I have done for you?" he asked them. "You call me 'Teacher' and 'Lord,' and rightly so, for that is what I am. Now that I, your Lord and Teacher, have washed your feet, *you also should wash one another's feet*. I have set you an example that you should do as I have done for you.**
>
> **I tell you the truth, no servant is greater than his master, nor is a messenger greater than the one who sent him. Now that you know these things, you will be blessed if you do them."**
>
> **John 13:12-17** NIV

The gospel hasn't changed. It is still the same. Jesus is still calling believers to wash feet, which is symbolic of serving others with a heart of humility.

In the days of Jesus' ministry on earth, the people wore sandals, and their feet got dirty. When they arrived at their destination, it was natural for a servant to wash their feet. Jesus did that for His disciples, setting an example for us to *serve one another*. "Service" is a characteristic of God's mighty men and women in this hour.

Paul couldn't do it alone. There were many places to go and many people to see. He cared about all of the people, and he wanted to encourage them, uplift them, share with them, and hear their reports. He wrote half of the New Testament, but still, he could only be in one place at a time, ministering to a certain group of people. But he cared enough to say, "I'll send someone to you who has my same heart."

For Christians to simply get saved and sit in a pew, read their Bibles and pray, and go through life without any deliberate effort to touch other people, is to miss what Christianity is all about. This is why for so many people who are in the Church world today, Christianity is dead.

True Christianity is so contagious you can't help but share it. When the love of God gets inside of you, you will want to give His love away to other people, and when you give His love away, love will come back to you. When you share joy, joy will come back to you. You should be so excited about being a Christian that you don't think about wanting to do anything else but live for God every day of your life.

The Israelites had to get fresh manna each morning. If they kept it overnight and held on to it, it spoiled before the next morning. It's the same way with the Word of God. Share it while it is fresh in you!

God has a purpose for your life. You are here on this earth, not just to make a higher stack, but to share your life — the life of God that is on the inside of you — with other people.

Practical Application of a Servant's Heart

At a Christmas eve service at our church, I felt prompted to ask those who didn't have a place to go for Christmas day and who would be alone to come forward. Then I said, "How many members of the congregation are willing to take one of these people into your home and have them for lunch for an hour or two and share your Christmas with them?"

The wonderful thing is, people responded with compassion and all of the people who came forward had a place to go for Christmas. No one spent Christmas day alone.

After the service was over, a lady said, "This is true Christianity." True Christianity is visible. It isn't just an idea, a philosophy, or a theological opinion. Christianity is something you can measure, you can feel, you can see. What happened on that Christmas eve should be happening all the time.

Jesus said, **"By this all will know that you are My disciples, if you have love for one another"** (John 13:35). In other words, there will be no question about the way you care for each other.

Jesus said we're not to hide His light that's in our lives under a bushel, but **"Let your light so shine before men, that they may see your good works and glorify your Father in heaven"** (Matthew 5:16).

You Need To Touch Hurting People

A person with a servant's heart is a person who is submissive and obedient to authority, spiritually and naturally;

he is sensitive and caring, diligent and fully committed to the Lord.

If we are going to effectively reach and minister to all the people who are in need, it will take millions of believers rising up with the heart of a servant.

As you look at a church, you might think everything is okay, but many people are hurting. Some are going through divorce. Others are going through bankruptcy. Others are challenged with sickness or disease. Great needs exist in the church as well as outside the church.

We are dealing with a generation of hurting people, perhaps hurting worse than any other generation in history, because we have the accumulative effects of broken marriages, drugs, alcohol, violence, and rejection. Heaped on top of this is the media invasion of people's minds.

If the army of God will get out of the barracks and get on the battlefield, we can reach hurting people. It's time for God's team to get off the bench and get into the game!

It's going to take the personal ministry of the Holy Ghost flowing through every believer in these last days. That does not diminish the offices of the pastor, evangelist, prophet, apostle, or teacher, but it does enlist all believers for service.

If we are going to touch people's lives, it will require time and effort. Some people have said, "God has never spoken to me to become involved in the work of ministering to other people." Are you ready? Hear the Word of the

Lord: **"...you are My disciples, if you have love for one another"** (John 13:35).

Philippians 2:1-4 NIV says:

> **If you have any encouragement from being united with Christ, if any comfort from his love, if any fellowship with the Spirit, if any tenderness and compassion, then make my joy complete by being like-minded, having the same love, being one in spirit and purpose. Do nothing out of selfish ambition or vain conceit, but in humility consider others better than yourselves. Each of you should look not only to your own interests, but also to the interests of others.**

What Are You Doing for Others?

In the fall of 1971, sitting on my bed in a dorm room at a state college in Arkansas, the Lord asked me, "What have you ever done for others?" That was a turning point in my life when I realized that all my life -- my job, the pursuit of an education, and my involvement in sports -- were all for me. I wept with tears of repentance as I realized my selfishness. God turned my heart outward to other people.

Jesus said, **"Greater love has no one than this, than to lay down one's life for his friends"** (John 15:13).

In John 21:15-17, Jesus had fixed a meal for His disciples on the lake of Galilee after His resurrection. After they had eaten, He spoke to Simon Peter:

> **"Simon, son of Jonah, do you love Me more than these?" He said to Him, "Yes, Lord; You know that I love You." He said to him, "Feed My lambs."**

He said to him again a second time, "Simon, son of Jonah, do you love Me?" He said to Him, "Yes, Lord; You know that I love You." He said to him, "Tend My sheep."

He said to him the third time, "Simon, son of Jonah, do you love Me?" Peter was grieved because He said to him the third time, "Do you love Me?" And he said to Him, "Lord, You know all things; You know that I love You." Jesus said to him, "Feed My sheep."

Based on what Jesus said, *do you love Him*? How much are you feeding His sheep? It's time to recognize, you are either into Christ or into religion. You are either into living for God or living for yourself.

What was Jesus really saying to you and me? "If you love Me, feed My sheep — My little ones, My big ones, and My medium-sized ones. Be concerned about the interests of other people, giving them something that will last for all eternity."

10

JESUS — ULTIMATE EXAMPLE
OF SERVANTHOOD

In this hour, I believe there is a desperate need for the Body of Christ to have a fresh understanding of the importance of serving others. In His life and ministry, Jesus gives us the ultimate example, model, or pattern of a true servant.

> **Let this mind be in you which was also in Christ Jesus.**
>
> **Philippians 2:5**

In this verse, *mind* means "attitude, purpose, or heart." The kind of heart, mind, purpose, and attitude Jesus had is described in verses 6-11:

> **Who, being in the form of God, did not consider it robbery to be equal with God.**
>
> **Philippians 2:6**

Colossians 1:19 says, **"For it pleased the Father that in Him** [in Christ, the Son] **all the fullness should dwell."**

John 1:18 says, **"No one has seen God at any time. The only begotten Son, who is in the bosom of the Father, He has declared Him."**

The Son, Jesus Christ, was the closest to the Father. God the Father allowed all that was in the Godhead to be revealed through His Son on the earth. Jesus didn't think it robbery to be counted equal with God, but notice the attitude He took.

> **But made Himself of no reputation, taking the form of a bondservant, and coming in the likeness of men.**
>
> **Philippians 2:7**

Jesus was full of glory, power, honor, dominion, and might. He was high and lifted up and seated at the right hand of God, the Father. He had angels all around Him, yet for a season, He left all that to humble Himself and take on the form of a servant. He was made in the likeness of men.

Now, that may not mean much to you since you are already made in the likeness of a man or woman, but in the beginning, Jesus was not made in the likeness of man. He allowed that to take place in Bethlehem in a little stable when He was laid in a manger. That was a decision of His will to allow Himself to be formed and fashioned and go through everything that we would go through, even the birthing process, and grow up as a child. It was a humbling, humiliating experience, but Jesus did it.

Jesus didn't take upon Himself any reputation. When He came, it was the shepherds who honored Him. The great ones of the earth didn't come. He didn't have a great reception in the sense that most kings would have if they left heaven and came to earth. He was made of absolutely no reputation.

> **And being found in appearance as a man,** *He humbled Himself* **and became obedient to the point of death, even the death of the cross.**
>
> **Philippians 2:8**

He humbled Himself is a key phrase. People sometimes talk about God humbling them, but victory and blessing come in our lives *when we humble ourselves.*

God had called Jesus to accept our sin. We know that Jesus Christ was slain before the foundation of the earth, so it was in God's heart and mind that redemption would be worked out through His Son, and He was called to Calvary. In that moment in Gethsemane, Jesus cried out, **"Father, if thou be willing, remove this cup from me: nevertheless not my will, but thine, be done"** (Luke 22:42 KJV).

Jesus became obedient unto death. It was a humiliating death, one of excruciating pain by crucifixion.

> **Therefore God also has highly exalted Him and given Him the name which is above every name,**
>
> **That at the name of Jesus every knee should bow, of those in heaven, and of those on earth, and of those under the earth,**
>
> **And that every tongue should confess that Jesus Christ is Lord, to the glory of God the Father.**
>
> **Philippians 2:9-11**

In God's Kingdom, the way up is down. The way to be blessed is to give. The way to receive is to release. God's laws work exactly opposite of the world's laws. The world says if you are going to go higher, step on people. God says if you are going to go higher, serve the people around you. If you are going to gain, you must be willing to give up what you have. Then you will receive true riches.

The world says, "Get all you can and can all you get." But God says, "Be willing to give it all up, because then I will give you what no man can give you."

As believers, we are sons and daughters of God. It is the Father's good pleasure to give us the Kingdom. We have been raised up and seated together with Christ in heavenly places. We walk upon the high places of the earth, and the enemy has been put under our feet. We know that we have authority to remove mountains (of challenge) through prayer, through the name and the blood of Jesus, through the power of the Holy Spirit, and through the spoken Word of God.

So how do these privileges correlate with a servant heart? When Jesus came, the Jews anticipated a political Savior Who would deliver them from the bondage of Roman domination. The Zealots were looking for someone who would take up their cause and liberate them from the terrible bondage and oppression they were under due to unjust taxation and as literal slaves of the Roman state. When Jesus came, they thought He was the Messiah scripture spoke of Who would rule with a rod of iron.

The Bible says that the Messiah would speak and

nations would be consumed and that all peoples of the earth would bow down to Him at Jerusalem. Isaiah prophesied that these things would happen. The people anticipated it, and in their minds, they could see themselves being a part of it. They couldn't wait for that day to come.

But Jesus came as Zechariah prophesied, riding on a young donkey, as a suffering, humble servant, the part of the Messiah they had not seen and did not understand. The prophets had spoken of Him, but it wasn't until later that Isaiah 53 was opened to them. He would be wounded for our transgressions. He would bear the iniquities of many. He would be rejected and despised.

We have been given authority and power over the enemy, but we have also been given the call to serve mankind. Jesus had authority over the devil. He said, **"...the ruler of this world is coming, and he has nothing in Me"** (John 14:30).

At the same time, He said:

> **But he who is greatest among you shall be your servant.**
>
> **And whoever exalts himself will be humbled, and he who humbles himself will be exalted.**
>
> **Matthew 23:11,12**

In 2 Peter 1:1, Peter opens his letter with, **"Simon Peter, a *bondservant* and apostle of Jesus Christ...."** In James 1:1, James opens his letter with, **"James, a *bondservant* of God and of the Lord Jesus Christ...."**

The Apostle Paul had great authority, power, dominion, and might. He knew that he was more than a conqueror through Christ and that he could do all things through Him. He knew that he always triumphed in Christ, yet in Romans 1:1, when he wrote to the church at Rome, he called himself, **"...a *bondservant* of Jesus Christ...."**

How do we reconcile the roles of *servant* of Christ and *friend* of Christ? Dominion, power, and authority, yet servanthood? We reconcile them in the Person of Jesus Christ. He left us an example that we are to follow. Paul expressed His example when he said, **"Let this mind** [attitude, heart, or purpose] **be in you which was also in Christ Jesus"** (Philippians 2:5).

Though Jesus had great power, dominion, and position, He humbled Himself. He identified with those around Him. He became obedient, even to the point of death on the cross.

You are a son or daughter of God by His choice. Jesus said, **"You did not choose Me, but I chose you and appointed you that you should go and bear fruit, and that your fruit should remain, that whatever you ask the Father in My name He may give you"** (John 15:16).

Servant by Choice

You are a servant by *your own choice*. Paul knew who he was in Christ. He knew who he was in the ministry. He knew he was called as an apostle, teacher, and preacher to the Gentiles, but it was *by his own choice* that he became a servant.

God chooses you to be His friend. He chooses you to be His son or daughter. He chooses His apostles, prophets, evangelists, pastors, and teachers. No man can take that honor unto himself. But we choose to be servants, because we have seen the example of Christ and the examples of His disciples.

In 1 Corinthians 9:19, Paul said, **"For though I am free from all men, I have made myself a servant to all, that I might win the more."**

One of the problems in marriages and families today is that many people have a "serve me" mentality! America is full of this mentality. Part of the problem in churches is that people come to be served. They go to church like they go to a restaurant.

We have a better smorgasbord at church than most restaurants! We have Living Bread and Living Water, manna from heaven. We are a part of Christ's Body, and God has called the Body to minister in service one to another. Paul said, **"...through love serve one another"** (Galatians 5:13).

In essence, Paul was saying, "You have been liberated, but you have not been set free to live in selfishness or in domination over others. You have been set free by God's love, and His love now fills your heart so you can love each other. The calling of every believer is to serve one another in Christ's love.

One of my staff members shared with me how a

115

Victory Bible Institute student (a veterinarian from Africa), had been ministering to a man in prison who didn't want to hear what he had to say. The VBI student had such compassion that he kept going back and sharing the love of Christ with the prisoner. He was rejected again and again, until finally, love broke through and the man responded to the message.

If you have an arrogant attitude and you are self-serving and someone you witness to throws it back in your face, you might take the position, "All right, buddy. That's it." But the VBI student kept going back to the prisoner. Each time he was rejected, but as a servant, he refused to be offended.

Why would a free man in the world serve a man behind bars? Some people in our society say, "Prisoners deserve to be locked up. They have committed crimes, so they ought to be there." But if we understand correctly, we were all behind bars and condemned to die before we were born again. We have all had the death penalty over us, for all have sinned and fallen short of the glory of God. If it wasn't for the grace of God, not one of us would be set free. Thank God that someone served the Lord by reaching out to serve us with the gospel of Christ!

James and John, the sons of thunder, wanted to call fire down on a Samaritan village that would not receive Jesus. They believed in the power message! They were heavy into using their authority. They said, "**...Lord, do You want us to command fire to come down from heaven and**

consume them...?" (Luke 9:54). In that moment, Jesus realized they had missed the whole point, so He rebuked them and said:

> "You do not know what manner of spirit you are of.
>
> "For the Son of Man did not come to destroy men's lives but to save them."
>
> Luke 9:55,56

Jesus also said, **"For God did not send His Son into the world to condemn the world, but that the world through Him might be saved"** (John 3:17).

It is encouraging when we look at the disciples and realize, there is hope for us! James and John were thinking, *Pretty soon Jesus is going to be in Jerusalem. He is going to knock off all the Romans, and we are going to be ruling with Him.*

They got a little word in: **"Grant us that we may sit, one on Your right hand and the other on Your left, in Your glory"** (Mark 10:37). Jesus had an answer for them, and He has an answer for us. They understood the power of heaven and their authority in prayer, but they thought it was so they could have some high position.

Jesus responded:

> "You do not know what you ask. Are you able to drink the cup that I drink, and be baptized with the baptism that I am baptized with?"
>
> They said to Him, "We are able." So Jesus said to them, "You will indeed drink the cup that I drink,

and with the baptism I am baptized with you will be baptized;

"But to sit on My right hand and on My left is not Mine to give, but it is for those for whom it is prepared."

And when the ten [other disciples] heard it, they began to be greatly displeased with James and John.

Mark 10:38-41

Greatness Comes with Serving

Mark 10:42-45 is a parallel passage to Philippians 2 where Jesus expressed the same thing Paul put into words after the cross, and that is, *greatness comes with serving.*

"You know that those who are considered rulers over the Gentiles lord it over them, and their great ones exercise authority over them.

"Yet it shall not be so among you; but whoever desires to become great among you shall be your servant.

"And whoever of you desires to be first shall be slave of all.

"For even the Son of Man did not come to be served, but to serve, and to give His life a ransom for many."

Jesus said, **"If anyone serves Me, let him follow Me; and where I am, there My servant will be also. If anyone serves Me, him My Father will honor"** (John 12:26).

Colossians 3:23,24 says:

And whatever you do, do it heartily, as to the Lord and not to men,

118

Knowing that from the Lord you will receive the reward of the inheritance; for you serve the Lord Christ.

What makes a church flow in the anointing of God? What makes the people happy? It is when people have a servant attitude.

When you haven't chosen to be a servant, little things will upset you. The attitude of a servant is, "My job is to serve, not to judge. I refuse to be offended by anyone or anything."

When you have the heart of a servant, you will pray for people to be saved. You will be willing to do whatever it takes to bring people to Jesus.

It is my observation that there is a selfish mentality in many people who have learned who they are in Christ, the revelation of prosperity, and their authority, power, and position. This side of the coin has almost blinded them to the other side: *It is by choice that we become servants.*

Why do we receive the gifts (or manifestations) of the Spirit? First Corinthians 12:7 says, **"...the manifestation of the Spirit is given to each one** *for the profit of all.*" We have been given the privilege of prayer that we might pray for one another. Romans 15:1 KJV says, **"We then that are strong ought to bear the infirmities of the weak, and not to please ourselves."**

Let's serve the Lord with a continual demonstration of compassion for others. It's a choice!

11

THE COST OF DISCIPLESHIP

"The cost of discipleship" refers to the cost of serving the Lord. Personally, I believe the rewards for serving the Lord far outweigh any cost.

Jesus had something to say about the cost of discipleship:

> Now it happened as they journeyed on the road, that someone said to Him, "Lord, I will follow You wherever You go."
>
> And Jesus said to him, "Foxes have holes and birds of the air have nests, but the Son of Man has nowhere to lay His head."
>
> Then He said to another, "Follow Me." But he said, "Lord, let me first go and bury my father."
>
> Jesus said to him, "Let the dead bury their own dead, but you go and preach the kingdom of God."
>
> And another also said, "Lord, I will follow You, but let me first go and bid them farewell who are at my house."
>
> But Jesus said to him, "No one, having put his hand to the plow, and looking back, is fit for the kingdom of God."
>
> Luke 9:57-62

Jesus did not soft-pedal the demands and requirements to be His disciple. His requirements were very strong, stringent, and demanding. Nowhere in Scripture did Jesus ever recant on what He called people to do or on anything He said. One of the teachings we have needed to bring the stability, diligence, and consistency in the Body of Christ is the message of "the cost of discipleship." The rewards far outweigh the cost. God blesses us with righteousness, peace, joy, victory, and eternal life.

When I look back at the things I gave up to follow Christ, I'm glad I left them! There are people who have not yet totally sold out to God because they have not understood what He is asking of them. They haven't entered into the total benefits, blessings, and joy. There are things they have held on to, because they haven't understood that Jesus came to give them life in abundance (John 10:10).

Matthew 16:24 says **"...If anyone desires to come after Me, let him deny himself, and take up his cross, and follow Me"** I have found the best way to be blessed and to prosper is *to do what Jesus said on all counts.*

With this explanation, let's look into the Word from Luke 9 and examine how Jesus responded to the three individuals He called to follow Him.

"I Will Follow You Wherever You Go"

The first man said, **"Lord, I will follow You wherever You go"** (Luke 9:57). He was excited and enthusiastic. Jairus's daughter had been healed, the centurion's servant had been miraculously healed, Jesus had stilled the tempest, He had preached in Capernaum, He had preached in His hometown, the paralytic had been healed, the loaves and fishes were multiplied, and numerous miracles had been manifested. Obviously, Jesus had a number of people around Him who were following Him.

There were so many following Jesus who wanted to do more than just eat loaves and fishes that Jesus **"...appointed seventy others also, and sent them two by two before His face into every city and place where He Himself was about to go"** (Luke 10:1).

A whole crowd of people were ready to receive the loaves and fishes, they were ready to hear the message, but then, there were others who chose to be disciples — who decided not only to hear His Word, but to continue in it.

A *disciple* is "one who receives with the intent, purpose, and decision to go and share with others."

John 8:31 says, **"...If you abide in My word, you are My disciples indeed."** To be a disciple takes a commitment to obey the commands of Jesus Christ and to daily abide in His Word.

Each day we are to do what Jesus said to do. His way is

better than ours. To do what He says is not a heavy burden. It is not oppressing. His yoke is easy, and His burden is light (Matthew 11:30).

Jesus said, **"And you shall know the truth, and the truth shall make you free"** (John 8:32). Disciples are free people. They are people who have continued in the Word to the point they have put it into practice in their personal lives and it has liberated them. The mighty warriors God is calling in this hour are liberated so they can liberate others.

When Jesus initially began to call the disciples, He invited them to His house. He grew up in Nazareth, a short distance from the coastal cities along the Sea of Galilee. He could go back to His mother's house in Capernaum around the sea coast area. We have reason to believe that He could have stayed in the home of James or John, and He probably did stay in Peter's house, because we read where He healed Peter's mother-in-law who was sick of a fever.

We know that the week before His crucifixion, Jesus was in Bethany, just a couple miles over the Mount of Olives from Jerusalem. He was staying in the home of Mary, Martha, and Lazarus.

Yet, Jesus said, **"Foxes have holes and birds of the air have nests, but the Son of Man has nowhere to lay His head"** (Luke 9:58). What did He mean by this?

It is obvious that a fox has a place that belongs to him,

and the birds have a place that is theirs. The meaning of this verse is that regardless of where Jesus went, ultimately *He was rejected. He had no place of acceptance.* John 1:11 says, **"He came to His own, and His own did not receive Him."**

I believe Jesus' response to the man who said he would follow Him anywhere went something like this: "Are you ready for rejection? Are you ready to experience the ostracism of the cross, of not being received because of the message we preach?"

When you look at the population of the world, even the population of America, the majority of the people of the world have not accepted Christianity.

At Church Growth Conferences all across the country, I have asked, "How many people in your community are saved?" Most responses indicate that 20 to 30 percent or less are born again, whether they are talking about New York, the East coast, the West coast, the South, or the Midwest. We are in a society that hasn't fully embraced Jesus Christ. Many people have a form of religion, but I am talking about those who are rightly related to the resurrected, living, healing, saving, and delivering Jesus!

Nazareth had no problem with Jesus for thirty years. He was a nice man. He went to the synagogue every day. The problems came when the miracles started happening and when the message started coming forth. Then Jesus was rejected.

Perhaps you have had to separate yourself from people who rejected you so you could go on with Christ.

The Bible says, **"The fear of man brings a snare..."** (Proverbs 29:25). Many people are afraid of being rejected. One of the most severe psychological attacks you can experience is to be rejected.

We have to make a decision of whether to confess Jesus Christ publicly or to be closet Christians. You must decide whether His life will be exhibited publicly in your family and you will go through the rejection, or whether you will just continue to be a secret service Christian. It is time to take a stand and say, "I am going to be a disciple, and I am going to lift Jesus Christ up in the marketplace. I am going to lift Him up on my job."

The rejection and persecution won't come until you lift up Jesus. Jesus calls us to make a public decision, for He said, **"...whoever is ashamed of Me and My words, of him the Son of Man will be ashamed..."** (Luke 9:26). Paul said, **"...I am not ashamed of the gospel of Christ..."** (Romans 1:16).

"Let Me First Go and Bury My Father"

To the second man in the passage we read from Luke 9:59, Jesus said, **"Follow Me."** This man responded, **"Lord, let me first go and bury my father."** That's an important thing to do in our society. Jesus said, **"Let the dead bury their own dead, but you go and preach the**

126

kingdom of God" (v. 60). It sounds to me like Jesus was pretty urgent about His call. *It takes a sense of urgency to be a disciple of Jesus Christ.*

The pull of family will keep some people from obeying Jesus to become a disciple. In many cases, the sense of urgency doesn't override the commitment to their family.

Jesus is speaking of something deeper and broader than just the funeral service. He is talking about, "Will you be committed and sold out to the Kingdom of God?" Jesus isn't going to contradict or violate the commandment, "Honor your father and your mother," the first commandment with promise. But He had called this man to go preach, and he is between two decisions: to go and take care of that need, or to go and preach the Kingdom of God.

The Lord spoke to me that I was to preach my father's funeral when he was killed in an accident. It didn't violate a higher calling from what the Lord had told me to do. It was a word from His Spirit. People who had never been in church heard the gospel that day, and as we gave an altar call for people to receive Christ, many responded.

We have to make a decision. Are we going to obey God? What has God called us to do? He has called us to put the Kingdom of God first. But if a man destroys his family, does not provide for them, and doesn't love his wife, it is very difficult to preach the gospel before other people. In other words, we need to live the gospel in the home.

Many people have never settled the issue of which comes first — God or family. Many people say, "The family was the first institution." I say, "In the beginning was *God*." God takes priority.

We have a calling that's higher than anything else on the earth, and it comes from God the Father, to serve Him, to love Him, and to honor and worship Him.

I went through an Abraham-Isaac type of test when God called me to go to O.R.U., and leave a full athletic scholarship at a state college in Arkansas. No one encouraged me to obey God. In fact, just the opposite happened. People visited me and told me why I shouldn't go. I made a decision to obey God.

Sharon faced a similar test when I graduated from O.R.U. and she still had one year to complete. We had opportunities to go to other cities and minister with Youth for Christ. Sharon finally came to a point of commitment where she said, "If I have to give up my education to go and preach the gospel, I will do it."

Jesus said, **"But seek first the kingdom of God and His righteousness, and all these things shall be added to you"** (Matthew 6:33).

Sometimes people have tried to save their marriage by neglecting the Kingdom of God. It will never work, because they have broken the laws of God. They say, "I know God has called me to go to the mission field, but because of my family, I need to stay here." If you will obey

God and take your family with you, He will bless every area of your life.

If you are forsaking the Kingdom of God to keep something, you will lose it. If you give it for the Kingdom, God will give it back to you.

"Let Me First Go and Bid My Family Farewell"

When Jesus asked the third man in the scripture from Luke 9:61 to follow Him, the man said, **"Lord, I will follow You, but let me first go and bid them farewell who are at my house."** Jesus said to him, **"No one, having put his hand to the plow, and looking back, is fit for the kingdom of God"** (Luke 9:62).

The third man Jesus called lacked *singleness of purpose.* God's call takes priority over everything, whether it's a profession, a career, or a family's desires.

Sharon and I Sold Out to God

When Sharon and I were dating and we were talking about getting married, I asked her, "Honey, are you willing to go to Africa and live in a mud hut? The Lord might call us there, and we must be willing to go." Then I said, "I don't want an answer right now. I want you to think about it for a week."

I know I was naive and young at the time in the way I presented it, but on the other hand, as I read the Scriptures,

I understood the principle that we had to be fully sold out to whatever God called us to do.

When we started Victory Christian Center, it cost us everything. We laid everything on the line. We did it in the midst of intense criticism. When the Lord said to me, "Go for it," we never looked back.

We gave up everything to start the church. We would do it again if we had to. In fact, about that same time, we sold our only car to pay a ministry bill in a situation that resulted from someone else's mistake. We were pastoring a new church, Victory Christian Center, and we didn't own a car. But a good name was more important to us than wheels.

A few thousand people were coming to the church, and we didn't have a car, all because of the stand we had taken to be current on all bills. The Lord spoke to a man in our body who owned a used car dealership, and he loaned us a car.

A few days later, my brother Charles who was in the Air Force, called, not knowing what we were going through, and he said, "We are moving from one air base to another, and we need to leave one of our cars with you for several months. Could you keep it?" We said, "Well, we just might be able to do it!" Hallelujah!

God's Provision Is More Than Enough

When Jesus appointed the seventy disciples and sent them out two by two, He said:

"The harvest truly is great, but the laborers are few; therefore pray the Lord of the harvest to send out laborers into His harvest.

"Go your way; behold, I send you out as lambs among wolves.

"Carry neither money bag, knapsack, nor sandals; and greet no one along the road.

"But whatever house you enter, first say, 'Peace to this house.'

"And if a son of peace is there, your peace will rest on it; if not, it will return to you.

"And remain in the same house, eating and drinking such things as they give, for the laborer is worthy of his wages. Do not go from house to house.

"Whatever city you enter, and they receive you, eat such things as are set before you.

"And heal the sick there, and say to them, 'The kingdom of God has come near to you.' "

Luke 10:2-9

What did Jesus mean when He said, **"Carry neither money bag, knapsack, nor sandals..."**? Was He saying, "Do without. Take a poverty vow"? No, He was saying, "Travel light, because I will take care of you. I will provide."

Remember the rich young ruler who asked Jesus what he had to do to inherit eternal life (Mark 10:19-22)? He was too bound by his possessions to become a disciple of

Jesus Christ. Jesus didn't say to him, "Let me make you a better deal." Jesus let him walk away.

Now, this is a part of Christianity that a lot of people don't understand. They can't see Jesus letting people walk away because of John 3:16. Salvation is for all. The free gift is to whoever will call upon the name of the Lord, yet Jesus let this guy, who expressed his desire for eternal life, to walk away and didn't say anything else. Jesus didn't pursue him, He didn't try to persuade him, He simply let him go. Why? Because there was one thing that stood between that young man and receiving the gospel: *he loved his possessions more than God.*

God said in the Ten Commandments, **"You shall have no other gods before Me"** (Exodus 20:3).

Jesus said:

> **"Hear, O Israel, the Lord our God, the Lord is one.**
>
> **"And you shall love the Lord your God with all your heart, with all your soul, with all your mind, and with all your strength." This is the first commandment.**
>
> **Mark 12:29,30**

To be a disciple of the Lord Jesus Christ means we will have *nothing* between Him and us. *He is number one in our lives.*

Rewards for Following Jesus

Jesus admonished the disciples about being bound to riches. He also gave an encouraging word about the rewards of leaving all to follow Him.

"How hard it is for those who have riches to enter the kingdom of God!"

And the disciples were astonished at His words. But Jesus answered again and said to them, "Children, how hard it is for those who trust in riches to enter the kingdom of God!

"It is easier for a camel to go through the eye of a needle than for a rich man to enter the kingdom of God."

And they were astonished, saying among themselves, "Who then can be saved?"

But Jesus looked at them and said, "With men it is impossible, but not with God; for with God all things are possible."

Then Peter began to say to Him, "See, we have left all and followed You."

So Jesus answered and said, "Assuredly, I say to you, there is no one who has left house or brothers or sisters or father or mother or wife or children or lands, for My sake and the gospel's,

"Who shall not receive a hundredfold now in this time — houses and brothers and sisters and mothers and children and lands, with persecutions — and in the age to come, eternal life."

Mark 10:23-30

Some of the disciples left everything. When James and John were at their nets, and Jesus said, "Follow Me," they left their nets and forsook their father.

Some people might say, "Don't you think they should

have arranged for someone else to take over the business and allowed a few weeks to make the transition?"

Many people won't accept Jesus' call, because they have heard a watered-down Christianity that has adjusted to modern society. But God's call to disciples has never changed, and His rewards are far greater than the cost of discipleship.

When God called me to go to Oral Roberts University and prepare for ministry, it was very difficult for my parents to let me go. They didn't want me to go, because initially they didn't understand why I would leave a full college scholarship to go to O.R.U. My girlfriend, who is now my wife, didn't want me to go. My football coach didn't want me to go. There are times when you have to leave the people who want you to do that which is contrary to what God has spoken.

I can remember dealing with several circumstances. Some of the students on the state college campus told me that because O.R.U. believed in healing and speaking in tongues, it was of the devil. The devil threw every kind of roadblock he could to keep me from making that decision.

I'm saying that, not in any way to draw attention to myself, but sometimes when someone preaches leaving all to follow Jesus, people think, "Sure, but you've never done it, so how can you say that?" I haven't done all that the disciples did, but there are things I have done that are very similar.

One of the benefits some people have had in this hour is they have grown up in Christian homes with people who are supportive of their decision to follow Christ. Ultimately, once my family realized I was going to O.R.U., they blessed me and helped me get through school. Praise God!

Mark 10:31 says, **"But many who are first will be last, and the last first."** It may look like you are last, but if you put Jesus Christ first, you will go to the head of the class!

If you have left all to follow Christ, be encouraged and don't look back. God will give you fathers, mothers, children, and people who will stand with you. I have found it to be so.

12

You Ought To Be Teachers

The writer of Hebrews, thought to be Paul, said he had many things to share about Jesus beyond the fact that He was likened unto the high priest, Melchizedek. But he said it was hard to express them because the people were *"dull of hearing"* (Hebrews 5:11 KJV).

Dull of hearing means you have become "spiritually calloused, unable to comprehend, receive, or accept the Word."

> For when for the time *ye ought to be teachers*, ye have need that one teach you again which be the first principles of the oracles of God; and are become such as have need of milk, and not of strong meat.
>
> For every one that useth milk is unskilful in the word of righteousness: for he is a babe.
>
> But strong meat belongeth to them that are of full age, even those who by reason of use have their senses exercised to discern both good and evil.
>
> Hebrews 5:12-14 KJV

"When for the time ye ought to be teachers" means there is a growth process in the normal maturity of a Christian. You should grow spiritually over a period of time to the point where you become a teacher. You should mature to the point where you are no longer just simply on the receiving end, but you become a giver, imparting information and ministry.

The maturing process from milk to meat may be different for each person, but the writer of Hebrews says, **"When for the time ye ought to be teachers."** He doesn't say, "When for the time *you have an option as to whether or not you would like to be a teacher."*

That is an expectation from God. It isn't an invitation; it is a command that in the growth process of a Christian, we reach the point where we become concerned about other people, realizing we have something to give.

That doesn't mean we will stand behind a pulpit, go to the mission field, be an evangelist, teach seminars, or teach in school, but every believer can communicate in his own way what he knows about God.

Some people say, "I can't articulate well." The truth is, some people will relate to you better than to someone else.

I want to challenge you, *"You* ought to be a teacher." You ought to be headed toward the age of maturity as a teacher. Either you are there now and you need to make a decision to obey God, or you need to realize, "It's normal for a little baby to grow up and become mature. It's abnormal for a child to be wearing diapers at age twenty!"

There are Christians wearing spiritual diapers who have been Christians twenty or thirty years, and they have never grown up to maturity. It's time to get out of the Romper Room and go on to maturity!

The goal of our spiritual lives should be that we become reproducers. God told Adam and Eve, **"...Be fruitful, and multiply, and replenish the earth, and subdue it..."** (Genesis 1:28 KJV). God is speaking something very similar to the Body of Christ today: *Multiply and replenish the earth with spiritual children.*

In the Great Commission Jesus said, **"Go therefore and make disciples of all the nations..."** (Matthew 28:19). He didn't say, "Make students." You can be a student without being a disciple. He didn't say, "Come on, you twelve students and go with Me." He called them *disciples.*

A disciple is one who receives from a person so he can reproduce what he learns in others. A disciple learns for the purpose of imparting to another person. In other words, discipleship is a never-ending process. We haven't completed the learning cycle until we begin to give out to others what we have learned.

You may be a believer, but it is possible you are not a disciple. You may receive Christ and know Him, but you may be wearing spiritual diapers because you haven't grown enough to receive strong meat. Strong meat is for those who will impart what they have to others.

Everyone wants to receive the strong meat of the Word, the revelation, the deep truths. But strong meat is for those who are teaching, ministering, and giving out. Every believer can impart truth.

Someone Discipled Me

One of the men who imparted the most truth in my life was a young man I worked with in the oil fields when I was first saved.

This young man, Ricky Erwin, was studying to be an engineer during the school year, and in the summer we worked together. He was four years older than me, and every day on the back of that pickup or at lunch, he would talk to me about what God was doing in his life. He would ask me questions, and he would let me ask him questions.

I've learned from a lot of people, but this young man taught me as much about God as anyone I know. He wasn't a preacher or a missionary. He was an average Christian who was willing to share what he knew.

Share What You Know

We need to shake off the mentality that if you're not a preacher, you don't have anything to share. Or, if you have not gone through Bible school, then you can't talk to anyone about God. You can share what you know. If all you know is John 3:16, someone needs to hear it.

When I first got saved, all I knew was the Four Spiritual Laws, and the summer after I worked in the oil fields, the Lord said, "Now that you have been taught, it is time for you to start sharing." I said, "Lord, who do You want me to share with?" He said, "Get all the children together at the boys' club and teach them."

I asked, "What am I going to teach them?" Inside of me the thought came, "Teach them the Four Spiritual Laws." Every week all summer long, I taught the same lesson:

1. God loves you;
2. You are a sinner separated from God;
3. Jesus died for your sins; and
4. You must receive Jesus Christ.

Those boys heard the same lesson every week. I didn't know any more, but that's what they needed to hear. Just as importantly, I needed to share something. I don't know whether you can do it in your office, on coffee break, in your neighborhood, before work, after work, or at night with a few people, but I do know, *God will plant you in a place to share if you are willing to obey Him.*

Skillful in the Word of Righteousness

God is saying, "How long are you going to stay a baby? When are you going to grow up? When are you going to get to the place of maturity in your life where you are called to be?"

For every one that useth milk is unskilful in the word of righteousness: for he is a babe.

Hebrews 5:13 KJV

You must be skillful in the word of righteousness. *Righteousness* is a gift of God in which He gives us "right standing with Himself." When Jesus Christ died on the cross and shed His blood, He paid for our sin, cancelling it out. He gives His righteousness to us in exchange for our sin when we accept Him as our personal Lord and Savior.

Righteousness frees you from guilt, condemnation, fear, and inferiority. If a person has guilt and condemnation hanging over his life, he is unskillful in the word of righteousness.

If you are skillful in the word of righteousness, which means you are moving out of the baby stage into maturity, that means the devil can't lay a number on you, a guilt trip, or a condemnation trip for past sins. The mature person refuses to accept condemnation and guilt.

The person who is skillful in the word of righteousness won't be afraid. When you know that you are right with God and every barrier *between* you and God has been removed, you are God's child and you a joint-heir with Jesus Christ. You are linked up with Him, and you are a partaker of His divine nature. In this position, no one can stand against you. If God is on your side and you have His favor, then righteousness will do a work inside of you so that you realize no weapon formed against you will prosper.

Isaiah 32:17 says, **"The work of righteousness will be peace, and the effect of righteousness, quietness and assurance forever."** When you are skillful in the word of righteousness, you won't be in turmoil. You may face situations that bring tribulation, but inside, you know you are in right relationship with God and the effect of righteousness brings quietness and peace.

The person who is skillful in the word of righteousness won't feel inferior. If you know you are in right relationship with God, then you know you are no longer down on the bottom, but you are lifted up.

A few years ago, as we ministered in one of the government-subsidized housing projects in north Tulsa, our witnessing teams went to one couple who had lost their jobs, their house, and their cars. Poverty had gotten a firm hold on them.

The husband later told us, "When the witnessing team came to our door, I didn't want to let them in, but something told me to do it. They began to talk to me about Jesus and how God could forgive me, cleanse me, and give me a new start. I didn't want to hear it, but then I accepted it."

His wife said, "I was in bed at 1:00 in the afternoon, because I had nothing to live for." Although they were on the bottom in their lives, they accepted Jesus Christ.

Each week, the team went back into their apartment community and taught them principles from God's Word. This couple joined our church. God restored their jobs, house, and cars; and today, they are ministering the gospel, sharing Jesus Christ with the broken, the hurting, and the downtrodden. They have grown in the word of righteousness and are now sharing the strong meat of the Word with others.

The word of righteousness will revolutionize your life. It will supernaturally lift you out of despair and negative circumstances. You will no longer be a babe, but you will rise to maturity. At that point, you will have something to share with others.

Many people will not share their faith or talk about what God has done because of fear. They haven't developed in the word of righteousness.

God is for you. He will do for you what He has done in my life. He will help you, and He will use you to minister to others.

A few years ago, a group of our teenagers went to Harlem and to the Bronx. They had prepared a drama ministry that dealt with gut-level issues of life — drugs, abortion, and immorality. They brought people to the point where they could accept Jesus Christ. Our teenagers grew more that summer giving out what they had on the inside of them than in all the years we had been putting the Word in them. What am I talking about? *Strong meat is for those who will give out of themselves to bless others.*

Many people are always looking for deep revelation, meat, or truth – something they have never heard taught before. They are ever learning, but never coming to the knowledge of the truth, always wanting "a new thing."

I believe the deepest truth in the entire Bible is found in John 3:16: **"For God so loved the world...."** If you opened your Bible to John 3:16, many Christians would say, "That's elementary. We've already heard that." Yet, the love of God is the deepest revelation of all!

When does the Word become meat to us? When we put it into practice and begin to give it out to others.

Strong meat belongs to those who have their senses exercised to discern between good and evil. That's the gift of righteousness, but then there are the *acts of righteousness*.

When you live righteously, it means you avoid evil. You live according to God's commandments. Maturity is the ability to discern between good and evil and to refuse the evil and choose the good.

There are millions of people who commit evil and call it good and look at that which is good and call it evil. There are people who want to get Christianity off of television, because they believe it is evil and it is corrupting our nation.

This happened in our public schools several years ago when a few people said, "Preaching Christianity should not be allowed in the public school system." As a result, laws were passed saying no one could openly preach Christianity (or share Jesus) in public schools. Thank God for those who have taken a stand to uphold the word of righteousness and who are working to reverse such decisions.

Strong Meat from the Woman at the Well

In John, chapter 4, Jesus had gone to Jacob's well. He talked to a woman who had had five husbands and was living with a man to whom she was not married. He began to reveal to her the need for living water in her life and that He had living water to give her. When He revealed that He was the Messiah, she believed Him.

She ran back into the city to tell others to come and meet Him. His disciples, who had gone into the same town to get something to eat, hadn't witnessed to anyone. They just went to get some food, and when they returned, they saw Jesus talking to this Samaritan woman, a sinner.

> **And at this point His disciples came, and they marveled that He talked with a woman; yet no one said, "What do You seek?" or, "Why are You talking with her?"**
>
> **The woman then left her waterpot, went her way into the city, and said to the men,**
>
> **"Come, see a Man who told me all things that I ever did. Could this be the Christ?"**
>
> **Then they went out of the city and came to Him.**
>
> **John 4:27-30**

They all came to hear Jesus, because of one woman who, in the natural, didn't have the proper credentials to share Jesus! Everyone in the town knew her reputation, yet she witnessed of Jesus.

> **In the meantime His disciples urged Him, saying, "Rabbi, eat."**

But He said to them, *"I have food to eat of which you do not know."*

John 4:31,32

What is the strong meat Jesus ate? Verses 33 and 34 define this meat:

Therefore the disciples said to one another, "Has anyone brought Him anything to eat?"

Jesus said to them, "My food [*The King James* says, "meat"] is to do the will of Him who sent Me, and to finish His work."

Jesus was ministering out of what He had, giving it to a woman who was in need. You will never get on the strong meat of God's Word until you begin to give it out. Then your spirit will digest that meat, and you will grow spiritually.

Soulwinning

Jesus said:

Do you not say, "There are still four months and then comes the harvest"? Behold, I say to you, lift up your eyes and look at the fields, for they are already white for harvest!

John 4:35

Jesus was talking about soulwinning. He was talking about ministering to hurting people.

I believe we have "played church" long enough. When people are saturated with the Word, but they don't give it out, usually they will hop from church to church. It has nothing to do with the minister. It has to do with their acting on the Word of God. Strong meat will begin to come into your life as you share what you know with others.

It's time to obey the Bible and begin to grow up. It is time for the world to be reached. We are not going to reach it if, when we learn about God, we sit and hold onto what we have. As we take what we have received and share it with others, evangelism will go on.

Parable of the Talents

Let's examine the account of the parable of the talents in Matthew 25:14-30:

> For the kingdom of heaven is like a man traveling to a far country, who called his own servants and delivered his goods to them.
>
> And to one he gave five talents, to another two, and to another one, to each according to his own ability; and immediately he went on a journey.
>
> Then he who had received the five talents went and traded with them, and made another five talents.
>
> And likewise he who had received two gained two more also.
>
> But he who had received one went and dug in the ground, and hid his lord's money.
>
> After a long time the lord of those servants came and settled accounts with them.
>
> So he who had received five talents came and brought

five other talents, saying, "Lord, you delivered to me five talents; look, I have gained five more talents besides them."

His lord said to him, "Well done, good and faithful servant; you were faithful over a few things, I will make you ruler over many things. Enter into the joy of your lord."

He also who had received two talents came and said, "Lord, you delivered to me two talents; look, I have gained two more talents besides them."

His lord said to him, "Well done, good and faithful servant; you have been faithful over a few things, I will make you ruler over many things. Enter into the joy of your lord."

Then he who had received the one talent came and said, "Lord, I knew you to be a hard man, reaping where you have not sown, and gathering where you have not scattered seed.

"And I was afraid, and went and hid your talent in the ground. Look, there you have what is yours."

But his lord answered and said to him, "You wicked and lazy servant, you knew that I reap where I have not sown, and gather where I have not scattered seed.

"So you ought to have deposited my money with the bankers, and at my coming I would have received back my own with interest.

"Therefore take the talent from him, and give it to him who has ten talents.

"For to everyone who has, more will be given, and he will have abundance; but from him who does not have, even what he has will be taken away.

"And cast the unprofitable servant into the outer darkness. There will be weeping and gnashing of teeth."

We will lose what we have unless we learn to use it to build God's Kingdom. We will lose the knowledge we presently have from the Word of God unless we are willing to share it.

When Jesus gave the Great Commission to go and make disciples, it was a command.

Jesus said, **"If anyone desires to come after Me, let him deny himself, and take up his cross, and follow Me"** (Matthew 16:24).

It isn't a call to some easy life. Neither was it easy for Jesus to go up Calvary's hill for you and me, but He did it because of love. That's the same reason we are to go on to maturity and share Jesus with others.

13

WILL *YOU* ANSWER GOD'S CALL?

He who wins souls is wise.

Proverbs 11:30

Daniel 12:3,4 says:

Those who are wise shall shine like the brightness of the firmament, and those who turn many to righteousness like the stars forever and ever.

But you, Daniel, shut up the words, and seal the book until the time of the end; many shall run to and fro, and knowledge shall increase.

We are living in this time right now. We are living in a time where we can leave one part of the earth one day, travel all the way across the earth and return in a couple of days. Travel, knowledge, and information have increased.

In 2 Peter 3:7-9, the Spirit of God spoke through Peter:

But the heavens and the earth which are now preserved by the same word, are reserved for fire until the day of judgment and perdition of ungodly men.

But, beloved, do not forget this one thing, that with the Lord one day is as a thousand years, and a thousand years as one day.

The Lord is not slack concerning His promise, as some count slackness, but is longsuffering toward us, not willing that any should perish but that all should come to repentance.

It may seem like the day of the Lord is coming very slowly, that God is slack and holding back, but this Word says the reason that Jesus has not yet come is *because of God's mercy*. God is giving sinners time to repent. His will is for all to repent. **"The longsuffering of our Lord is salvation..."** (2 Peter 3:15).

While Christians want Jesus to come, Jesus wants us to go and share Him with others so they will be saved.

What will it take for world evangelization? It will take the removal of selfishness. That's the bottom line. First, the Church must give financially to support missions. Then people must give up their lives for the call and the cause of Jesus Christ.

God said to Isaiah, **"Whom shall I send, and who will go for Us?"** Isaiah responded, **"Here am I! Send me"** (Isaiah 6:8). That takes the laying down of your life and your own agenda.

There is no question but what we are in the time of the end. The two areas we can focus our attention on are Europe and Jerusalem.

Europe will be the place of the rise of the Roman Empire once again. It is interesting that the European Economic Community has already brought nations together that will form the foundation of the empire over which the Antichrist will rule.

At the same time, Jerusalem will become more and more the cup of trembling Zechariah prophesied it would be. All nations are turning against Israel, and there will be constant pressure for peace. The Bible says that Israel will one day give in, but the peace will be short-lived.

We see all these things happening. What does it mean? It means we need to get with the program and go after souls!

A few years ago, doors began to open in Eastern Europe. Many places where the gospel couldn't go are now wide open, and God is sending out the call: *Who will go? Who will answer that call?*

Third world nations are praying for Christians to come because we have the gospel, the literature, and the training for revival that is so desperately needed in their countries.

The mile relay, as I knew it, was four laps around the track. Four different runners were given the baton. The first one took it and ran. A strong runner always starts out to get a good position. The second and third runners must run strategically, but the key to winning the relay race is *the last runner.*

In centuries past, the torch or the baton has been carried by others before us. Those who had the fire — Abraham, Moses, David, and John the Baptist, for example

— passed the torch on. Jesus came, making it very clear what the race was all about.

Martin Luther, John and Charles Wesley, Billy Sunday, and other great leaders rose up. But now we're in the final lap of the race.

You always save your best runners for the last lap. The fastest, strongest, and most anointed generation will be this generation.

There will be an outpouring and a running with the baton like never before. The good news is, *you* and I are called to participate in the race. Will *you* answer God's call?

Wake up! The baton is being passed to you. *Heaven is on its feet!* Lay aside every weight and sin. Keep your focus on Jesus, and **"press on toward the goal to win the [supreme and heavenly] prize to which God in Christ Jesus is calling us upward"** (Philippians 3:14 AMP).

PERSONAL PRAYER OF COMMITMENT

Yes, Lord, I will answer the call to become equipped to carry the baton of revival wherever You would have me go. I lay down my life anew this day, Father, for Your perfect will to be done in me, in Jesus' name.

I accept Your Son Jesus Christ as my personal Lord and Savior. I accept the exchange of the filth of my sin for His righteousness, purchased at Calvary.

Lord, cleanse my heart and renew a right spirit within me. Give me eyes to see and ears to hear others, both sinners and saints, as You see and hear them. Give me the tongue of the learned to know how to speak a word in season to those who are hurting, to lift, strengthen, and encourage them in You, Lord.

Do a thorough work in me, Holy Spirit, so I can be a reproducer of divine live in the earth in this hour, in Jesus' name. Amen.

_____

(Signature)

_____

(Date)